T0254996

Lecture Notes in Computer Science   13799

Founding Editors

Gerhard Goos
Juris Hartmanis

The series Lecture Notes in Computer Science (LNCS), including its subseries Lecture Notes in Artificial Intelligence (LNAI) and Lecture Notes in Bioinformatics (LNBI), has established itself as a medium for the publication of new developments in computer science and information technology research, teaching, and education.

LNCS enjoys close cooperation with the computer science R & D community, the series counts many renowned academics among its volume editors and paper authors, and collaborates with prestigious societies. Its mission is to serve this international community by providing an invaluable service, mainly focused on the publication of conference and workshop proceedings and postproceedings. LNCS commenced publication in 1973.

Luca Foschini · Spyros Kontogiannis
Editors

Algorithmic Aspects
of Cloud Computing

7th International Symposium, ALGOCLOUD 2022
Potsdam, Germany, September 6, 2022
Revised Selected Papers

 Springer

Editors
Luca Foschini 🆔
University of Bologna
Bologna, Italy

Spyros Kontogiannis 🆔
University of Patras
Rio, Greece

ISSN 0302-9743   ISSN 1611-3349 (electronic)
Lecture Notes in Computer Science
ISBN 978-3-031-33436-8   ISBN 978-3-031-33437-5 (eBook)
https://doi.org/10.1007/978-3-031-33437-5

This Springer imprint is published by the registered company Springer Nature Switzerland AG
The registered company address is: Gewerbestrasse 11, 6330 Cham, Switzerland

Preface

The International Symposium on Algorithmic Aspects of Cloud Computing (ALGO-CLOUD) is an annual international symposium that aims to tackle the diverse new topics in the emerging area of algorithmic aspects of computing and data management in modern cloud-based systems interpreted broadly to include edge- and fog-based systems, cloudlets, cloud micro-services, virtualization environments, decentralized systems, as well as dynamic networks.

The symposium aims at bringing together researchers, students, and practitioners to present research activities and results on topics related to the algorithmic, design, and development aspects of modern cloud-based systems. ALGOCLOUD is particularly interested in novel algorithms in the context of cloud computing, cloud architectures, as well as experimental work that evaluates contemporary cloud approaches and pertinent applications. ALGOCLOUD also welcomes demonstration manuscripts, which discuss successful system developments, as well as experience/use-case articles and high-quality survey papers.

Topics of interest included (non-exclusively):

- Analysis of Algorithms and Data Structures
- Algorithms for Decentralized Systems
- Algorithms for Dynamic Networks
- Game-Theoretic Approaches for Cloud Computing
- IoT and Cloud Computing
- Fog and Edge Computing
- Resource Management and Scheduling
- Data Center and Infrastructure Management
- Privacy, Security and Anonymization
- Cloud-Based Applications
- Virtualization and Containers
- Performance Models
- Cloud Deployment Tools and Their Analysis
- Novel Programming Models
- Storage Management
- Economic Models and Pricing
- Energy and Power Management
- Big Data and the Cloud
- Network and Graph Analysis
- Network Management and Techniques
- Caching and Load Balancing
- Machine Learning for Cloud Computing and Systems
- Cloud Computing and Systems for Machine Learning

ALGOCLOUD 2022 took place on September 6, 2022, in Potsdam, Germany. It was part of ALGO 2022 (September 6–10, 2022), the major annual congress that combines the premier algorithmic conference European Symposium on Algorithms (ESA), along with a number of specialized symposia and workshops, all related to algorithms and their applications, making ALGO the major European event for researchers, students, and practitioners in algorithms and their application.

There was a positive response to the ALGOCLOUD 2022 call for papers. The diverse nature of papers submitted demonstrated the vitality of the algorithmic aspects of cloud computing. All submissions went through a rigorous peer-review process and were reviewed by at least three Program Committee (PC) members. They were evaluated on their quality, originality, and relevance to the symposium. Following their recommendations, the PC accepted six original research papers covering a variety of topics that were presented at the symposium. We would like to thank all PC members for their significant contribution to the review process.

Finally, we would like to thank all authors who submitted their research work to ALGOCLOUD and the Steering Committee for its continuous support.

We hope that these proceedings will help researchers, students, and practitioners understand and be aware of state-of-the-art algorithmic aspects of cloud computing, and that they will stimulate further research in the domain of algorithmic approaches in cloud computing in general.

April 2023   Luca Foschini
                                                               Spyros Kontogiannis

Organization

Steering Committee

Spyros Sioutas	University of Patras, Greece
Peter Triantafillou	University of Warwick, UK
Christos D. Zaroliagis	University of Patras, Greece

Symposium Chairs

Luca Foschini	University of Bologna, Italy
Spyros Kontogiannis	University of Patras, Greece

Program Committee

Dimitris Amaxilatis	Spark Works Ltd. & University of Patras, Greece
Paolo Bellavista	University of Bologna, Italy
Javier Berrocal	University of Extremadura, Spain
Cristian Borcea	New Jersey Institute of Technology, USA
Ioannis Chatzigiannakis	University of Rome "La Sapienza", Italy
Luca Foschini	University of Bologna, Italy
Antonio Galletta	University of Messina, Italy
Spyros Kontogiannis	University of Patras, Greece
Isam Mashhour Hasan Al Jawarneh	University of Bologna, Italy
Ulrich Meyer	University of Frankfurt, Germany
Domenico Scotece	University of Bologna, Italy
Spyros Sioutas	University of Patras, Greece

Contents

Cloud-Based Urban Mobility Services

Spyros Kontogiannis[1,2] (iD), Paraskevi-Maria Machaira[2], Andreas Paraskevopoulos[1,2],
Konstantinos Raftopoulos[2], and Christos Zaroliagis[1,2(✉)] (iD)

[1] Computer Technology Institute and Press "Diophantus", Patras University Campus, 26504
Patras, Greece
[2] Computer Engineering and Informatics Department, University of Patras, Patras, Greece
{kontog,machaira,paraskevop,kraft,zaro}@ceid.upatras.gr

Abstract. We present a cloud-based ecosystem for urban mobility services that
involves citizens, authorities, corporations, resources, and services, all working
together towards a common well-being. Our goal is to have a platform that allows
the exploitation of shared mobility-related data sources by harmonically cooperating mobility-related services, and at the same time smoothly balances the computational load across the full cloud continuum. Towards this goal, we present
the relevant orchestration mechanisms, both at service level and at cloud substrate level, which take into account particular characteristics per mobility service,
and real-time performance measurements and availability of computational nodes
within the cloud substrate. Moreover, our ecosystem allows the migration of both
data segments and source-code segments within the cloud infrastructure, towards
optimizing an objective for the entire ecosystem's performance and sustainability. Our core services are based on novel algorithmic approaches that are deemed
necessary for providing real-time query responses.

Keywords: sustainable mobility · multimodal route planning and navigation ·
crowdsourcing · resource sharing · incentives · parking/delivery services

1 Introduction

Urban mobility plays a pivotal role in meeting the objectives of economic competitiveness, social cohesion, and sustainable growth. An efficient transportation system should
be at the heart of a human-centric city. The stereotypical approach of building and
expanding the provided infrastructure (e.g., public transport, parking spaces, etc.) over
and over, can't solve all the challenges related to mobility, since the urban environments
gradually tend to a saturation point with respect to the management of public spaces. It is
now more than evident that sophisticated approaches are required to focus on optimizing
the utilization of the existing infrastructure. Moreover, it is also clear that mobility is
a poly-parametric challenge, not just about developing transport infrastructure and services, but also about overcoming the social, economic, political, and physical barriers,
and considering the interaction with citizens, and dependence from resources of other
types of services. For instance, urban mobility is not necessarily only about transport, but
it also accesses core socio-economic services like health, education, and employment.

© The Author(s), under exclusive license to Springer Nature Switzerland AG 2023
L. Foschini and S. Kontogiannis (Eds.): ALGOCLOUD 2022, LNCS 13799, pp. 1–20, 2023.
https://doi.org/10.1007/978-3-031-33437-5_1

Therefore, mobility services should be integrated and interact with numerous other types of services related to urban well-being, such as parking, delivery, and sharing, in an urban ecosystem providing to citizens an entire arsenal of everyday services, opportunities and resources. For example, citizens do not only commute with public transport, but they also exploit other means of transportation such as private cars, or car/bike/bicycle sharing, in an unprecedented blend of all possible means of transport. Moreover, they also share resources (e.g., private parking spots, their own vehicles, or even some of their own time) in support of services (e.g., parking, vehicle sharing, delivery, etc.) for other individuals.

Nevertheless, a prerequisite for having this tremendous blend of diverse urban well-being services work smoothly together, would be to create a more sophisticated urban ecosystem than a mere collection of technological advancements. For example, the consideration of the human-in-the-loop is a crucial aspect for the discovery and exploitation in real-time of available shared resources (e.g., shared parking spots, pick-up and drop-off points for shared vehicles on the move, ongoing or scheduled delivery tasks), before requesting the commitment of a new resource. As another example, non-fixed-route public transport is affected, to a certain extent, by the traffic conditions which are also affected by other parameters, such as either scheduled or unforeseen political/cultural/commercial events involving many people, mobility with one's own means, weather conditions, etc. Finally, other quite challenging urban services such as on-demand delivery of goods, require access (as supporting services) to, but also affect the quality of, the provided services by the mobility platform.

All these directly interacting (existing or envisioned, for future deployment) urban services to the citizens, can only co-exist in a holistic urban-life orchestration ecosystem, that will be based on a volatile, scalable, and efficient computing environment, such as a cloud architecture, and will also allow the exploitation of crowdsourced information and crowdfunded/shared resources. This ecosystem will provide novel business opportunities, such as the commercial exploitation of private parking spaces (e.g., of supermarkets, when they are closed), but also a better utilization of idle sources and human involvement, before considering the deployment of new resources, infrastructures, and extra human power.

The goal of this paper is to showcase a pragmatic application scenario of such a holistic urban ecosystem, based on a volatile and scalable cloud-based infrastructure, that involves citizens, authorities, corporations, resources, and services, all working together towards a common well-being.

The rest of this work is organized as follows. Section 2 presents related work in cloud-based architectures. Section 3 presents the architecture of our cloud-based ecosystem for mobility services. Section 4 and Sect. 5 present the frontend APIs and the backend, respectively, of the mobility services. Section 6 presents the orchestration of the backend mobility services. Section 7 discusses the data aggregation and analytics methods of our ecosystem. Section 8 presents the cloud-substrate orchestrator of our ecosystem. We conclude in Sect. 9.

2 Related Work in Cloud-Based Architectures

Over the last years, Cloud Computing has played a dominant role in the implementation of massive-scale and complex data computing systems. This is the main reason why many Cloud-based architectures have arrived at the forefront to confront many challenges that appeared since the era of the IoT. On the other hand, a variety of IoT devices with some embedded intelligent applications penetrates our lives and have some very demanding requirements like real-time processing and responding back to the end-users, which the solution of Cloud Computing cannot always manage efficiently.

To settle down such demanding requirements of the IoT devices many technologies have been developed over the last years. For instance, cloudlet, fog computing and mobile edge computing that follow the concept of the *Edge Computing* paradigm. Its idea is to handle the majority of the computing processes and the storage requirements of the end-devices to some nearby servers which belongs to the edge network. Edge Computing satisfies largely the requirements of the latency-sensitive IoT applications, because of the location of the edge network that makes the network latency to get significantly reduced. Another aspect of these IoT devices is that they are resource-constrained and they typically have some fixed embedded software/applications that bring in some difficulties to provide cross-platform on-demand services. Hence, to eliminate these challenges and also to use in parallel the reduced processing and storage capabilities of the end devices, the concept of *Transparent Computing* is introduced (Zhou and Zhang 2006) (Ju Ren 2017) (Zhang et al. 2020) in combination with Edge Computing, proposing a new IoT based architecture.

The Transparent Computing paradigm entails the isolation of the software from the hardware level of the related devices. More specifically, all the software components like Operating Systems (OS), applications and development tools are deposited to the server side in the edge or the cloud network and managed centrally, while the computational process is performed on the end-devices. That simply means that the scalability of the IoT devices is increased and allow users to extend their functionalities by fetching (using streaming) every time from the servers the necessary code blocks and the related OSes that are needed. Additionally, by having knowledge and understanding of the constraints that the devices usually present and at the same time their real time requirements, a transparent computing-based architecture can take advantage of the processing power of the edge servers by sending the more demanding tasks to them.

The proposed transparent computing-based IoT architecture is illustrated in Fig. 1. The architecture consists of five layers, in which the Edge Server Layer plays a dominating role. It tries to confront the problems of providing real-time and context-aware data processing while at the same time tries to satisfy the need of dynamic provision of on-demand applications and services to the end devices. This architecture is multi-beneficial, since it provides reduced response delay (by enabling data analytics and service provisioning at the edge), context-aware service support (by fully utilizing local computing and storage), centralized resource management (services and data are stored and maintained in edge/cloud servers but are managed centrally), cross-platform and on-demand service provisioning (by decoupling the hardware and software of the IoT devices, and by loading desired services and underlying OSes on-demand from the edge servers), and enhanced functional scalability (by enabling IoT devices to load the suitable drivers and services from the edge servers).

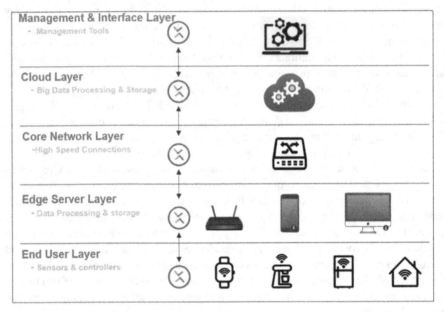

Fig. 1. A transparent computing-based IoT architecture

To illustrate the proposed architecture, a case study regarding the implementation of a transparent computing-based lightweight wearable, called TCwatch, is presented in (Ju Ren 2017).

TCwatch is embedded with a lightweight hardware, provides scalability, and loads different third-party services on-demand from the edge server, which is implemented by a smartphone. In this case study the TCwatch fetches all the required applications and OSes from the smartphone, if they are stored locally. Otherwise, the smartphone fetches all the applications and the OSes from the cloud, where they are also stored. The edge and the cloud servers are also used for computational processes.

Although this case study concerns a preliminary implementation, the evaluation of its performance is noteworthy, since the TCwatch reduces latency by 60.70–85.50% and energy consumption by 67.60 – 91.20% in dynamic App execution in relation to a traditional smart watch under different App sizes.

Another interesting related work concerns the Kubernetes *Edge Scheduler* (Toka 2021). Future applications over 5G technologies and beyond will pose requests for low-latency communication and ultra-reliability. In the aforementioned case study of TCwatch, we can realize that although the edge network can achieve strict delay criteria and low-latency communication between the end devices and the edge servers, it cannot meet the requirements of the application's reliability because the edge servers are generally prone to failures. Hence, in (Toka 2021), a Kubernetes orchestration tool, called

Kubernetes Edge Scheduler, is developed and ventures to expand its functionality to be suited for the edge network and to be able to fulfill the above requirements.

The Kubernetes Edge Scheduler schedules application components on the edge or the cloud network by considering first their latency requirements and the underlying network latency, and at the same time provides high reliability by offering back up resources for node failure cases.

The Edge Scheduler consists of three major components: the online-scheduler, the re-scheduler, and the node clustering component.

The *online scheduler* is responsible for the deployment of application components, called *Pods,* and the creation of the related *placeholders* (backup computing resources on edge nodes) by considering the Pod's delay and other computational criteria. A *placeholder* is computing backup resources on edge nodes that prevent the downtime of an application in case of a node failure by restarting the related Pods on it. It is crucial for the scheduler to create efficiently the placeholders in the system and always with respect of the Pod's latency requirements and the available resources that exist.

Another interesting characteristic that makes the Edge Scheduler robust is that its scheduling algorithm always strives to deploy the majority of the incoming Pod requests. Even in the case of lack of resources, the scheduler tries to free allocated resources on a specific node by migrating an already deployed Pod that can migrate without negatively affecting its smooth operation.

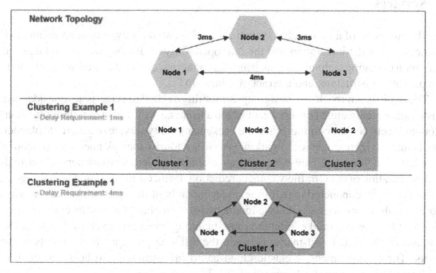

Fig. 2. Node Clustering example.

The *re-scheduler* (second component of the Edge scheduler) works to ensure the effectiveness of the resource's allocation. The re-scheduler works in an offline manner and tries to minimize the amount of the necessary placeholders in the system since as it is known, the edge network has limited resources. Hence, the careful reservation of the backup resources is one of the most critical steps, and it is also the reason for the importance of the re-scheduler component in the architecture.

The Node Clustering component of the Edge scheduler makes it able to work competently with large topologies, ensuring that the dynamic application placement and the network delay measurements scale effectively as shown in Fig. 2. More precisely, the solution creates hierarchically cluster layers of available nodes where each layer is built on a specific delay requirement. The clustering approach ensures that all nodes inside a cluster layer fulfill a distinct delay value. This practically means that the scheduling algorithm do not need to iterate the hole process through all the nodes of the cluster. After some evaluation experiments, we can conclude that the node clustering component benefits the process of the online scheduler and the re-scheduler in terms of the execution time.

To conclude, all the technologies mentioned in this section (Edge Computing and Transparent Computing) try to meet all the demanding requirements that the era of IoT applications have brought the last years, and to eliminate their difficulties in their application settings. Also, the adaption of the aforementioned technologies into new implementations, like the Kubernetes Edge Scheduler, can offer significantly improved results in relation to other classical technologies.

3 Architecture of a Cloud-Based Ecosystem for Mobility-Related Services

The development of a sustainable system for intelligent mobility, within an urban environment, needs the integration and the interoperability of diverse mobility-related services with emerging technologies such as interconnected commuters and vehicles, cloud computing infrastructure, and internet of things (IoT).

The typical approach for designing a mobility-related service is to consider it a master-slave architecture per service, in which a frontend API (e.g., a mobile application) intervenes between the commuter and the backend mobility service (e.g., a route planner, a real-time navigation service, a parking service, a tourist-tour planner, or a scheduler of orders to deliverers). However, modern mobility-related services depend on real-time aggregation of data (traffic/weather prediction, forthcoming events, accidents, etc.), which is usually conducted in real-time, independently of the specific mobility service. Moreover, these services should also interact with each other. For instance, a scheduler of delivery-requests would exploit the route-planning service as a subroutine, to assess in real-time the actual cost-metric between the different pickup/delivery points of the orders. The establishment of elastic cloud-based infrastructures to host master-slave architectures is not new (Rodrigues et al. 2017).

In this work our main goal is to consider the locality of data which are aggregated in real-time and are relevant for each of the services, as well as the determination of the computing requirements; that is, whether a particular backend service should be located at a remote, cloud server, a nearby edge computer supporting the service, or even our own terminal device (smartphone). For instance, in route planning in a metropolitan-scale environment, one could consider a scenario where a cloud server possesses all the (typically large) preprocessed information which are necessary for responding to arbitrary routing queries. On the other hand, local edge servers could also be employed, to serve routing/rerouting queries for commuters travelling in a particular (limited) geographical area. As for real-time navigation along an already precomputed route, such a task could be onloaded to the commuter's terminal device (e.g., a smartphone), provided that the necessary data (e.g., precomputed route and updated transportation subnetwork and map tiles) have already been prefetched or updated.

This type of locality-sensitive arrangement would lead to smaller network latencies (if at all necessary), a lot of computational effort held either at the edge or even at the terminal device, and only long-distance queries should be offloaded to the cloud-based routing server(s), since the nearby edge devices could not possibly possess the required data or computational power for serving them in acceptable response-times. Moreover, the deployment of a cloud-based infrastructure that hosts many mobility-related services, which are organized conceptually in master-slave architectures, would allow the exploitation of the same mobility-related information (e.g., real-time traffic conditions and prediction, demand for parking/commuting/delivery, weather conditions, etc.) which is aggregated via diverse data sources and require computationally intensive processing and storage.

At ultimatum, our goal is to have a platform that smoothly balances the load among harmonically cooperating mobility-related services, which goes beyond traditional cloud computing rationale that typically offloads heavy computational loads from the edges to the cloud, and exploits onloading of lighter computational loads to edges closer to the data sources, exploiting the locality of the edges to the individuals requesting the service and avoiding the excessive consumption of computational power by the cloud.

To showcase our rationale, we present in this work an ecosystem of individuals, legal entities, and services, targeting the common well-being of the entire urban environment. This ecosystem contains:

- Four mobility-related services: (i) route planning and navigation (RPN); (ii) tourist-tour planning (TTP); (iii) parking (PAR); (iv) delivery services (DEL).
- Three types of actors: individuals (e.g., commuters, tourists, deliverers); (ii) enterprises providing mobility-related information (e.g., parking vendors, route-planning servers, tourist-tour planning operators, delivery services vendors); (iii) public authorities (e.g., municipalities) regulating the ecosystem.

All these actors and services must be integrated and interact with each other, within a holistic urban-mobility ecosystem, in a trustworthy, secure, and privacy-preserving manner.

The overall architecture of the proposed ecosystem is shown in Fig. 3. It is worth noting that the logical structure of this ecosystem is that many frontend interfaces (mobile APIs for individuals, and dashboards for private vendors and public authorities) interact with a virtual backend consisting of all the necessary modules to support the envisioned services.

Apart from the above-mentioned conceptual architecture, in which all services are considered to operate in a master-slave manner, we proceed further to determine a more detailed vertical structure of implementation layers (cf. Fig. 4), each of which aims to determine a different level of refinement in the overall architecture.

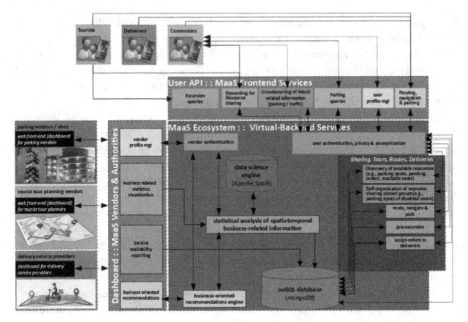

Fig. 3. Overall architecture for an Ecosystem of mobility-related services.

In this layered architecture, there is a vertical flow of information while serving specific queries. The top layer (Layer 5) provides all frontend APIs which interact with the actors of the ecosystem. Each frontend API then communicates with a virtual-backend service of Layer 4, which breaks down the service request into independent computational tasks that will jointly provide the response to the request. Each of these service-dependent tasks is then propagated to Layer 3, that will determine for it a group of eligible computing devices, depending on its computational requirements and the location of the necessary data for executing them. For instance, a routing task which needs updated traffic-related data for a particular neighborhood, may be allocated either to one of the cloud servers dedicated for the routing service over the entire urban area, or (if locality of the query permits this) to an edge device corresponding to the neighborhood within which the query should be accommodated, in case that the map is also split among edge devices on a per-neighborhood base. This matchmaking process will also take into account real-time data gathered in Layer 2. For example, in case of some emergencies (e.g., some unforeseen accident), for which only specific cloud servers are aware, affect a pending routing request, this should be reflected in the selection of the eligible computing devices for the corresponding tasks of this request.

The final allocation of each pending computational task to one of the eligible computing devices is then determined in Layer 1, where various performance indicators (e.g., already queued tasks and computational power per computing device, or current network latency estimations) are taken into account, not just for the particular task to be scheduled, but also for all the actively running tasks and the other pending tasks, possibly from other service requests that run in parallel within the ecosystem. The overall objective of the cloud-substrate orchestrator of Layer 1 may be the total throughput of the ecosystem, the energy consumption, or the overall environmental footprint (e.g., CO_2 emissions equivalent) for the computations, etc.

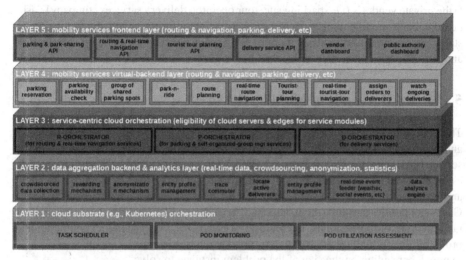

Fig. 4. Cloud-based infrastructure for the provision of mobility-related services.

4 Frontend APIs of Mobility Services

The proposed ecosystem integrates innovative mobility services, addressing the requirements for optimal routes, parking spots and delivery schedules by citizens, tourists, commuters, and deliverers, through consolidating parking-, traffic-, and availability-related information across all the transport modes (walking, embarking, disembarking, driving), means (car, bus, train, metro, ferry, airplane), parking spaces, and delivery service providers and workers. Each such service is implemented by a virtual-backend network service (Layer 4), which interacts with client-apps over the corresponding frontend API (Layer 5). The communication between them is performed by HTTPS using a lightweight and JSON-based request-response messaging pattern.

In Layer 5, all the required routing, parking, tourist-tour planning, or delivery parameters are collected by the frontend app, to construct and submit an appropriate query to the corresponding virtual backend service of Layer 4.

Layer 5 includes a set of frontend APIs for obtaining the corresponding spatio-temporal transport-aware data, user preferences and desired optimization criteria. In particular: a) the routing and real-time navigation API collects source, destination, departure time, parking locations for requesting optimal source-destination routes, and building the corresponding navigation directions; b) the tourist tour planning API collects source-destination locations, and personalized vacation-plan profiles for requesting optimal tour journeys; c) the parking and park-sharing API collects vehicle records, parking spot locations and capacities, for requesting parking reservations or parking spot sharing; d) the delivery service API collects the available deliverers, the pickup-delivery requests and a list of constraints for requesting a solution set of routes for each deliverer to carry out the requests; e) the public-authority dashboard collects modifications with respect to the public transport network status (e.g. traffic events, road accidents, itinerary delays); and f) the private vendor's (i.e., parking site, tour operator, delivery services company) dashboard collects modifications with respect to real-time information related to the service status (e.g. the real-time availability of parking spots, ticket and rental costs, availability and current positions of deliverers, etc.).

5 Virtual Backends of Mobility Services

There are four core virtual-backend services provided in Layer 4: the Route Planning and Navigation service (RPN), the Tourist-Tour Planning service (TTP), the Parking service (PAR), and the Delivery service (DEL). On a common basis, the services require as input the road, pedestrian and public transport network structure along with length and travel time metrics. Those are provided via the OSM (for road, pedestrian) and the GTFS (for public transport) input datasets. The RPN and PAR services can carry out their tasks in order of milliseconds. In contrast, TTP and DEL concern harder computational problems, therefore they may need to respond to queries in order of seconds, or even up to hours, depending on the size of the problem instance to solve.

5.1   Route Planning and Navigation Service

The RPN service is responsible for computing optimal time-dependent, multimodal and multicriteria (earliest arrival, minimum number of transfers, least walking time, vehicle type exclusions, etc.) source-destination routes, and for providing a real-time navigation along a precomputed route. It consists of the car routing subservice C-RPN (using OSM datasets) over road networks, and the public transport routing subservice P-RPN (using OSM and GTFS input datasets) over public transport and pedestrian networks. The routing is done by advanced algorithmic approaches, based on sophisticated extensions of Dijkstra's algorithm, such as the CFLAT oracle (Kontogiannis et al. 2017) and the ALT algorithm (Goldberg and Harrelson 2005). The fast response time is ensured by using cache-friendly data structures (sequence heap, data-compact and efficiently ordered vectors) and efficient heuristics (search-pruning and goal directed methods).

The overall functionality is carried out with a preprocessing (offline) phase generating traffic-related data structures and heuristic metadata, and afterwards with a routing query (online) phase, where the preprocessed heuristic metadata are exploited. The preprocessing is computationally demanding and thus should be conducted at dedicated routing cloud servers. These servers compute numerous optimal route trees from a set L of high importance nodes (e.g., highway hubs), called landmarks, in road and pedestrian networks. For each landmark $l \in L$, a set of the nearest stops/stations S_L and parking spots P_L are computed within secondary optimal route subtrees.

For each user query, providing a source point o, a departure time t_o and a destination point d, C-RPN and/or P-RPN compute a starting forward optimal route tree T_o from o, and a backward optimal route tree T_d from d within the underlying transport networks. The tree expansion is limited so that it includes small-sized sets L_o (within T_o) and

L_d (within T_d) of nearby landmarks from the source and the destination, respectively. Furthermore, depending on the type of the query, for each landmark the precomputed optimal route trees between landmarks, stops, parking spots, source point and destination point are added. Additionally, for computing time-dependent multimodal paths, P-RPN runs multi-source Dijkstra from the nearest stops S_{L_o} and/or parking spots P_{L_o} in the vicinity of the source, at the corresponding earliest arrival times to them, and/or multi-target Dijkstra to the stops S_{L_d} and/or parking spots P_{L_d} in the vicinity of the destination. The union of the optimal routes forms a subgraph consisting of the candidate optimal od-routes. Consequently, the routing algorithm post-preprocesses them, to choose those that minimize the user's objective function.

PRN also supports tasks of computing the nearest stops (by shortest walking time) to each GPS-generated track-point and, for each such stop, the list of available public transport itineraries within a requested time window.

5.2 Tourist-Tour Planning Service

The TTP service is responsible for computing complete packages of time-dependent tourist-tour solutions for visiting several places within a few days, starting from a source, and ending to a destination, in such a way that tourist's personalized preferences are satisfied as much as possible (this is the NP-hard Vacation Planning Problem). The service maintains a list of Points of Interest (POIs) consisting of tourist-attractive places, such as museums, monuments, etc.; and a list of user criteria (e.g., POI categories, intermediate destinations, journey and hotel residential duration, budget, etc.).

The tourist-tour planning algorithm, provided by the TTP virtual backend service, runs in two phases. In the first phase, it searches for candidate cities and the most interesting POIs per area, and then it designs daily itineraries in such a way to maximize the acquired aggregate user preference score from each POI, while distributing the available days of stay to the different intermediate destinations. In the second phase, the algorithm computes daily itineraries that consist of visits to the most interesting POIs accessible from the city centers (Tourist Trip Design Problem).

The algorithm uses a novel hierarchical and agglomerative-based clustering scheme, where each parent cluster is created by combining two child clusters. The next clusters to combine are those at minimum distance of their medoids. Each cluster is populated with metadata describing the POI members of the cluster, such as the sum of scores of all POIs, expected time to visit the cluster's POIs and expected score that will be gained if a tourist visits this cluster. The clustering is mostly static and thus, it is constructed during a preprocessing phase (i.e., offline). For guaranteeing performance, the offline cluster also keeps metadata that speed up the involved computations (e.g., to speed up the aggregate score computation per POI category). When the service is invoked, the backend is responsible for traversing the hierarchical clustering and finding the best nodes a tourist would most probably like to visit, considering the overall vacation duration (e.g., more days mean a greater area can be explored).

Also, the user preferences per POI category are considered, and that is done by a novel recursive algorithm based on dynamic programming. The main idea is to find a fixed number of itineraries visiting interesting locations, when the score and visiting time of each location is known. Since the Tourist Trip Design Problem is NP-hard, heuristics are employed. One such heuristic is the Iterated Local Search (ILS) algorithm, which can provide very fast high-quality solutions.

5.3 Parking Service

The PAR service supports the management of parking spaces that belong either to commercial parking sites, or to a self-organized closed group of commuters with their own shared parking spaces, (e.g., commuters with disabilities sharing within the group their own parking spaces). The service is responsible for the provision of real-time information to commuters about the availability of the parking spaces in the vicinity of a targeted location, and for handling parking space reservations on behalf of the commuters.

For the commercial parking sites, PAR is informed about the availability of parking spaces, upon the entry or the exit of a new vehicle. This is done either manually, via the parking site's dashboard (cf. Layer 5), or automatically (provided that the infrastructure of the parking site permits it). For the self-organized parking spaces, parking space owners inform PAR about the availability of their parking space interacting with the corresponding frontend API of Layer 5. PAR uses then the parking space availability information to serve requests for parking space reservations and/or cancelations of existing reservations.

5.4 Delivery Service

The DEL service performs optimal crew schedules for serving pickup-delivery requests. It solves a variant of the NP hard Vehicle Routing Problem, defining a realistic and advanced parameterization on several aspects of the problem. Its output is a set of feasible time-dependent pickup-delivery routes for each connected deliverer, which minimizes a customizable objective function (e.g., total travel distance), satisfying simultaneously the spatio-temporal constraints for the deliverers (e.g., work-shifts, starting/ending points, vehicle type and capacity), and for the orders (e.g., earliest pickup / latest delivery times, commodity capacity and required vehicle type for each good to be delivered, etc.).

A preprocessing step is required, involving the use of the RPN service, for computing optimal routes between each deliverer's starting/ending point, and each request's pickup/delivery points. Then the DEL backend service solves an appropriate mixed integer linear program using heuristic approaches (e.g., branch-and-bound, branch-and-price, or column-generation) to deal with the exponential search of the solution space. The basic approach includes a gradual expansion of a search tree where each node examines a subspace of the problem. The algorithm iteratively focuses on feasible solutions (schedules), keeping the currently best performing ones. To trace better solutions and integrate their subspace in the search tree, a dual linear integer program and a dynamic program (on dual LP reduced costs) are solved.

The DEL service provides both static schedules from scratch (when knowing all the orders and active deliverers beforehand) and dynamic reschedules (i.e., in online fashion) from a current feasible solution, to fit newly arrived orders. In the latter case, DEL receives in real-time the emergent order requests and/or the new deliverers. The DEL service also provides real-time tracking of the active deliverers who are currently serving some of the active orders.

6 Orchestration of Virtual Backend Mobility Services

The role of the orchestrators in Layer 3 of our ecosystem's architecture is to take over the mapping of the computationally demanding virtual backend services into independent tasks to be executed within the so-called Pods[1], and then determine all the eligible Pods per task, given the task's characteristics (computational demands, access to raw-data, relative location of each Pod, etc.).

Upon completion of all the independent tasks for a particular virtual backend service, the service itself acts as the reducer that collects the produced outputs and exploits them to respond appropriately to the submitted request. The distribution of the heavy computational burden per virtual backend service as uniformly among all edge devices and cloud servers as possible, demands some metadata to be generated and maintained, that will allow the execution of these tasks to these devices.

6.1 Orchestration of Route Planning and Navigation Service

We assume that the entire transportation network (multimodal, including walks and private cars) is divided into small (geographical) areas. The entire preprocessed data for responding efficiently to arbitrary routing queries are located at (one or more) cloud servers dedicated for the routing service. We also envision the use of dedicated routing edge devices, one per geographical area, possessing all the required preprocessed data for responding efficiently to queries which are confined in this area.

Upon arrival of a new query, a geographic 2D-grid is used to indicate a bounding box where the source and the destination are located. The spherical distance between source and destination (ranking into a low/medium/long range query), and the involved transport means, determine the computational requirements for the query at hand. If an edge device has the minimum CPU speed and memory requirements to respond to the query at hand, as well as the required preprocessed data within the specific bounding box, then a routing Pod residing at this edge would be considered as eligible for this task. On the other hand, if an edge device does not possess the required preprocessed data, or some unforeseen incident (e.g., a car accident that occurs in real-time) makes this preprocessed data temporarily invalid, the task must be served by a Pod residing at cloud server dedicated for the routing service.

Simple (unimodal, single criteria) public-transport routing queries can be carried out by a Pod residing at an edge device. More complex (e.g., multi-modal, multi-criteria) public-transport routing queries could be split into four tasks, to be executed possibly in different Pods, that involve: a) a forward optimal route tree T_o from the source o and the search for the nearest landmarks L_o, stops S_{L_o} and parking spots P_{L_o}; ;; b) a backward optimal route tree T_d from destination d and the search for the nearest landmarks L_d, stops S_{L_d} and parking spots P_{L_d}; ;; c1) the collection of a superset of the nearest stops $\overline{S}_{L_o} \supseteq S_{L_o}$ and/or parking spots $\overline{P}_{L_o} \supseteq P_{L_o}$ in the neighborhood of o, and a superset of the nearest stops $\overline{S}_{L_d} \supseteq S_{L_d}$ and/or parking spots $\overline{P}_{L_d} \supseteq P_{L_d}$ in the neighborhood of d, provided that all of them can be predetermined using spherical distance metrics; c2) the execution of multimodal-multicriteria profile queries, using: i)

---

[1] Collection of containers with shared storage and network resources (cf. Sect. 7).

each point in $\overline{S}_{L_o}$ and/or $\overline{P}_{L_o}$ as candidate intermediate source, where for each of them the time window of departure times can be predetermined using free-flow and congested travel time metrics, and ii) each point in $\overline{S}_{L_d}$ and/or $\overline{P}_{L_d}$ as candidate intermediate destination; and d) the integration of all optimal subroutes and the selection of the best combinations that constitute od-paths, based on user's objective function. The first three tasks can be computed independently of each other, possibly at different Pods. The last task should begin only after the completion of the other tasks, as part of the reducer's job for responding to the query at hand.

6.2 Orchestration of the Tourist-Tour Planning Service

The TTP service could be split in two task groups. The first group contains light (for short-range queries) to heavy (for medium-long range queries) tasks that can be carried out independently of each other. They can be distributed among all edge devices, the most appropriate probably being the ones closer to the tourist-tour related data (e.g., an edge device located at a tour-operator's office). Those tasks concern: searching POIs per city and user preferences, computing pairwise car/multimodal travel time profiles and journeys among POIs, clustering of POIs over cities and areas, and searching of clusters that match the user-defined preferences. The second group contains heavy tasks that can be carried out only when the tasks of the first group are finished. Those tasks concern computing optimal journeys over the preferred POI clusters and integrating and composing the best POI combinations into complete optimal tourist tour solutions.

For efficiently responding to arbitrary TTP queries, the entire transportation network along with the POI clusters is divided into (geographical) areas, and the preprocessed POI datasets are hosted in one or more cloud servers dedicated for the TTP service. Moreover, we envision the use of a dedicated edge device per geographical area, possessing all the required POI clusters per city, the tourist-aware criteria and ranking metadata, and the multi-modal travelling profiles that concern this area.

Upon arrival of a new TTP query, a hierarchical geographically based partition of the network and the user-defined vacation duration (radius) are used to indicate the candidate tour areas between source and destination. In that context, the spherical distance between source and destination, the vacation duration, and the estimated number of the involved POIs with respect to the user preferences predetermine the computational requirements for the query at hand. If an edge device has the minimum CPU speed and memory requirements with respect to computational demands of the query at hand, and all the required data within the candidate tour areas, then a Pod residing at this edge is eligible for carrying out the first-group tasks. Otherwise, the task should be sent to a Pod residing at a cloud server dedicated for the TTP service.

On the other hand, the second-group tasks, whenever they obtain the complete list of the candidate POIs and the optimal multi-modal routes between the POIs, can start the composition of the tour journeys and perform a search of the best ones in a parallel fashion.

6.3 Orchestration of the Parking Service

For the parking service, we consider a partition of the road network into small geographical areas, each one hosting lists of the available parking spots and sites, organized in categories (e.g., with or without washing, supporting or not individuals with special needs). The service includes management, reservation and sharing tasks of private/public parking spots and self-organized user groups that can be done independently per area and they can be hosted on multiple cloud servers without dependencies over the operations between them (excluding the pricing or rewarding synchronization tasks). Tasks of this kind have low computational requirements; thus, the eligibility is limited to data validity.

We also envision the use of a dedicated parking edge device per geographical area, possessing all the required updated data for responding efficiently to queries which are within this area. Upon arrival of a new query, if the parking edge device has a valid snapshot (with respect to the availability of the parking spots) within the required area, then a parking Pod residing at this edge would be eligible for this task. Otherwise, the task is sent to a Pod residing at a master cloud server dedicated for the parking service.

6.4 Orchestration of the Delivery Service

The DEL service is split into: a) routing tasks for obtaining the deliverers' optimal distances among the pickup and delivery points; b) solving tasks for finding the best optimal and feasible (based on constraints) routes within a specific search subspace (through search tree branches); and c) a cumulative task to integrate the optimal routes and select the best ones with respect to the defined objective function within the overall search space.

The solving tasks can begin when all routing tasks that concern the search subspace will have completed. The solving tasks focus on disjoint search subspaces and thus they can be carried out independently of each other. Both routing and solving tasks can be distributed uniformly among all eligible edge devices or/and cloud servers. The eligibility is in relation to the computational complexity and the data consistency and completeness. The solving tasks are computationally demanding; thus, only cloud servers are eligible to undertake them.

For responding efficiently to arbitrary order-scheduling queries, a cloud database maintains a full list of the deliverer starting/ending, pickup (stores, depots) and delivery (client) points and among them the shortest distances. If a query considers a point which does not exist in the database, or the computed shortest distance between a pair of points is outdated, then the routing subtask to be carried out requires an edge device or a cloud server with sufficient computational resources.

7 Data Aggregation and Analytics

Participation of end-users is crucial for the sustainability of a cloud-based ecosystem for mobility-related services. This is achieved in our case via a crowdsourcing mechanism (cf. Layer 2) that allows end-users to provide live-traffic information regarding emergencies (e.g., accidents, road works) as well as parking availability information. To ensure that the information provided by mobile users is reliable and of high-quality, we establish an incentive-based scheme that uses virtual credits (points) to reward users for providing truthful information. Apart from incentivizing truthful behavior, our rewarding scheme caters for point circulation, does not allow point over-accumulation, and prevents malicious users to aggregate points by misreporting.

Our ecosystem caters also for the active participation of commercial vendors and public authorities that provide parking services. It aggregates parking availability information for each individual parking site and creates its detailed business profile. Then, for a specific parking site P, it compares its business profile and geographic position with the corresponding business profiles of every other parking site in its vicinity and makes targeted business-oriented recommendations based on best practices of the similar parking sites. Comparing the performance, pricing policies and business plans of the parking sites of P's direct competitors, P's owner its prices, create special offers, add extra services etc., to make P more attractive to subgroups of more relevant in their own geographical area.

8   Cloud-Substrate Orchestrator

Our cloud-substrate orchestrator is based on Kubernetes[2]. Kubernetes is a powerful container orchestration platform, which has become the last years one of the most popular cluster managers. Its main functionality refers to the automated deployment, scaling and management of containerized applications which are deployed in the well-known components of Kubernetes, the *Pods*. Technically speaking, a *Pod* is a collection of one or more containers with shared storage and network resources and represents the smallest execution unit of Kubernetes.

Since it constitutes an open-source tool, we venture to reshape and expand Kubernetes functionality by giving transparency characteristics which improve the computation processes by avoiding transmitting massive data to the cloud servers, as they cannot possibly satisfy all the requirements of real-time applications due to the observed network latency, and there is a need to better explore the computational capabilities of edge and terminal devices within the cloud infrastructure.

In particular, to overcome the excessive overloading of remote cloud servers due to uncontrolled migration of raw-data towards them (a.k.a. off-loading), it would be more efficient for the users to adopt the migration of computational tasks (a.k.a. on-loading schemes) towards the raw-data sources, that would then be processed by nearby edge devices, so as to avoid network latency and improve user experience.

The motivation of the Transparent Computing (TC) is to isolate the computation and the storage for the servers and the terminals. We consider that all the software including Operating Systems (OSes), application programs and management tools are deposited on the server's repositories and can be easily loaded via the network during the execution on terminals (Zhang et al. 2020).

---

[2] https://kubernetes.io/

In our architecture, the software is run by Kubernetes Pods, which are located within the entire cloud infrastructure, including the edge devices. The advantage of the Kubernetes Pods is that we can easily replicate a Pod, so we can have a cluster of multiple replicas of the same software simultaneously on many nodes and that can make the user able to decide which device is the best one to offload the produced data. At the same time, all these Pods are bundled together under a Kubernetes service as shown in Fig. 5. By default, Kubernetes uses the service which is a way to expose an application running on a set of Pods as network.

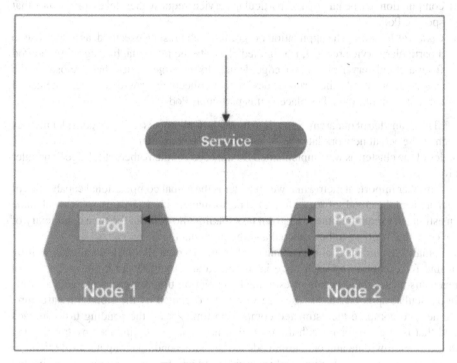

Fig. 5. Service Functionality

Exactly at this point our architecture intervenes to change the service's logic for the selection of a particular Pod to be served, among the Pods which are eligible for it. This gives us the ability to choose in real-time a specific Pod, located at a specific node, for the computation process that it needs to take place, based on the current measurements of all the alternatives for the execution of the service at hand. More specifically, with the contribution of the Kubernetes services, the scheduler can be informed during the orchestration phase about the available Pods and their locations in the cluster where these locations are represented by the nodes which are the target of the scheduler, and their characteristics (aka CPU, Memory) are crucial in order to choose finally the eligible Pod to offload the data and execute the request.

By considering our architecture, the terminals with the contribution of Kubernetes, and by considering some important metrics that we present later, we can determine an appropriate node within the cloud substrate hosting an execution Pod for the service, and collaborate with it, sending all the required data and/or the necessary code that are needed for responding to a service request, based on the following concepts:

- *Data Off-loading:* Migration of the missing service-related data, produced mostly in real-time, to a nearby edge device which already possesses the required Pod for the service at hand, or to a cloud server dedicated for the particular service. The computation on behalf of the particular service request then takes place into that specific Pod.
- *Code On-loading:* The application program which must be executed, as a response to a particular service request, is migrated closer to the raw-data, by migrating the Pod from a cloud server or another edge device, to the edge device that is closer to the raw-data, or even to the terminal device that collects the raw-data. Then, the actual service computation takes place at this particular Pod.

The main idea of our architecture is to make the Kubernetes rationale consider metrics such as the actual network latency, by measuring the communication delay between the nodes of the cluster, as was implemented for the needs of the Kubernetes Edge Scheduler (Toka 2021).

Another important metric that we consider is the actual computational capabilities of each node of the cloud substrate, like CPU performance characteristics, so as to calculate an estimated execution time for a given task, taking into account the time complexity of the code that is going to be executed and the input data.

Finally, our orchestration mechanism takes into account also the tasks already waiting in line for execution by each node in the cloud substrate. Overall, our orchestration mechanism uses the criterion of estimated completion time for each emergent service. In particular, upon arrival of a new service to be executed by the cloud infrastructure, we need to compare the estimated completion time for all the pending tasks in each Pod that is eligible for it, with the measured network latency induced by transferring the required raw-data and/or source-code to the corresponding computational (cloud or edge) device for the execution of this service, and add to this maximum the estimated execution time of the service at hand, to make the final decision for the allocation of the emergent service to a specific Pod like presented in Fig. 6.

After this computation that is implemented for each eligible Pod (and its hosting node) in the cloud, we can decide which is the best migration strategy to follow, i.e., an offloading or an onloading migration process, given the selection of the appropriate node and Pod to assign the service.

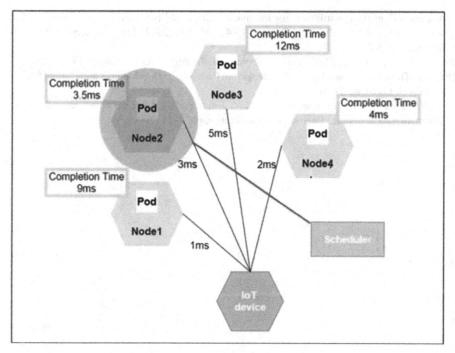

Fig. 6. Service Allocation to Specific Pod

9   Conclusions and Future Work

We presented a volatile, scalable, and efficient cloud architecture for materializing an ecosystem of mobility-related services involving a multitude of stakeholders. We showed how the necessary orchestration of various services across all layers of our cloud architecture can be executed. Our backend services are based on novel algorithmic approaches that are deem necessary for providing real-time query responses.

Acknowledgment. This work was supported by the Operational Program Competitiveness, Entrepreneurship and Innovation (call Research – Create – Innovate, co-financed by EU and GR) under contract no. T2EDK-03472 (project iDeliver).

References

Gavalas, D., et al.: Renewable mobility in smart cities: cloud-based services. In: IEEE Symposium on Computers and Communications (ISCC 2018), 1280–1285 (2018)

Goldberg, A.V., Harrelson, C.: Computing the shortest path: a* search meets graph theory. SODA **5**, 156–165 (2005)

Ju Ren, H.G.: Serving at the edge: a scalable IoT architecture based on transparent computing. IEEE Network 1–10 (2017)

Kontogiannis, S., Papastavrou, G., Paraskevopoulos, A., Wagner, D., Zaroliagis, C.: Improved oracles for time-dependent road networks (2017). doi:arXiv:1704.08445

Rodrigues, V.F., et al.: Towards enabling live thresholding as utility to manage elastic master-slave applications in the cloud. J. Grid Comput. **15**(4), 535–556 (2017). https://doi.org/10.1007/s10 723-017-9405-3

Toka, L.: Ultra-reliable and low-latency computing in the edge. J. Grid Comput. **19**, 31 (2021)

Zhang, Y., Duan, S., Zhang, D., Ren, J.: Transparent Computing: Development and Current Status. Chinese J. Electron. (2020)

Zhou, Y., & Zhang, Y.: Transparent computing: a new paradigm for pervasive computing. In: International Conference International Conference, pp. 1–11 (2006)

SQL Query Optimization in Distributed NoSQL Databases for Cloud-Based Applications

Aristeidis Karras[1], Christos Karras[1], Antonios Pervanas[1],
Spyros Sioutas[1], and Christos Zaroliagis[1,2(✉)]

[1] Computer Engineering and Informatics Department, University of Patras,
26504 Patras, Greece
{akarras,c.karras,pervanas,sioutas}@ceid.upatras.gr,
zaro@ceid.upatras.gr
[2] Computer Technology Institute and Press "Diophantus", Patras University
Campus, 26504 Patras, Greece

Abstract. A method for query optimization is presented by utilizing Spark SQL, a module of Apache Spark that integrates relational data processing. The goal of this paper is to explore NoSQL databases and their effective usage in conjunction with distributed environments to optimize query execution time, in order to accommodate the user complex demands in a cloud computing setting that necessitate the real-time generation of dynamic pages and the provision of dynamic information.

In this work, we investigate query optimization using various query execution paths by combining MongoDB and Spark SQL, aiming to reduce the average query execution time. We achieve this goal by improving the query execution time through a sequence of query execution path scenarios that split the initial query into sub-queries between MongoDB and Spark SQL, along with the use of a mediator between Apache Spark and MongoDB. This mediator transfers either the entire database from MongoDB to Spark, or transfers a subset of the results for those sub-queries executed in MongoDB. Our experimental results with eight different query execution path scenarios and six difference database sizes demonstrate the clear superiority and scalability of a specific scenario.

Keywords: Big Data and the Cloud · Query Optimization · SparkSQL · NoSQL databases · Indexes · Big Data Analytics for Cloud computing

1 Introduction

Data mining and analytics sectors have drawn much attention in our days by both academic and businesses communities in order to handle massive datasets. With modern libraries and existing systems such as Hadoop [4,30], which is a frequently used cloud platform for data mining, the efficient management of big

L. Foschini and S. Kontogiannis (Eds.): ALGOCLOUD 2022, LNCS 13799, pp. 21–41, 2023.
https://doi.org/10.1007/978-3-031-33437-5_2

data is no longer a promise. Several machine learning methods based on the MapReduce [14] architecture have gained popularity as they can be deployed on the cloud with the use of Apache Spark [6]. In contrast, when similar algorithms are implemented using MapReduce, intermediate results are written to the Hadoop Distributed File System (HDFS) [4] and read from there. However, this requires a considerable amount of time for disc I/O operations as well as vast amounts of resources for communication and storage.

Cloud computing can enhance analytics, machine learning, and other possible directions as the data are stored in a cloud provider and not locally. However, traditional relational databases face many challenges when employed in a cloud setting. There is a constant demand for high concurrent database read/write operations. In cloud computing, the complex demands of users necessitate the real-time generation of dynamic pages and the provision of dynamic information; as a result, the database concurrency rate is excessively high and tends to receive thousands of reading requests per second. It is difficult for a relational database to accommodate tens of thousands of SQL data write requests, and the hard drive cannot support the load. Additionally, there is a huge demand for the efficient storage and access of massive data. The massive data created dynamically, for relational databases in a cloud computing environment, has resulted in storing hundreds of millions of records in a table, making it exceedingly inefficient to execute an SQL query.

In contrast, complicated SQL queries that need multi-table lookup operations have led to the development of flexible systems such as the one presented here. In a system that contains massive amounts of data, we could issue several connected queries across big tables, intelligent data processing, and extensive data reporting. Although simple conditional paging queries on a single table with a primary key are often employed in cloud computing scenarios, they produce an extensive load to the environment, hence, we should seek for other options.

Despite the fact that the prevalence of relational databases (RDBMS) indicates that users often prefer making declarative queries, the relational method is inadequate for many big data applications. Initially, users want to extract, transform and load to/from multiple semi or unstructured data sources, which requires specialized programming. Secondly, customers might do complex analytics, such as machine learning and graph processing, which are difficult to be performed in RDBMS. Particularly, the majority of data pipelines shall ideally be defined using both relational queries and complicated procedural methods. Up to now, such kinds of systems, relational and procedural, have remained essentially separate, requiring users to choose between the two methods.

For the aforementioned reasons, we mainly focus in this work on distributed databases for query optimization including Spark SQL [6] and MongoDB [27] and show how to utilize both relational and procedural models in MongoDB and Spark SQL, using Hadoop [4,30,34]. With the use of a MongoDB connector for Apache Spark, the preceding connection occurs in order to perform speedy and complex queries. Spark SQL is an extension of Spark for structured data processing. Spark SQL allows users to effortlessly combine relational and procedural APIs, rather than requiring them to choose between the two. Furthermore, frameworks like Hadoop, Apache Spark, and Apache Storm [7], as well as distributed data storages such as HDFS and HBase [5], are gaining popularity since they are designed to make the processing of extremely massive volumes of data almost straightforward. Such systems appear to have a great deal of interest, and therefore, libraries (such as MLlib of Apache Spark) that enable the development and application of Machine Learning methods in the cloud are noteworthy.

Spark SQL bridges the gap between the relational and procedural models by contributing in two ways. Spark SQL offers a DataFrame (DF) API that may conduct relational operations on external data sources as well as the own distributed collections of Spark. MongoDB is utilized for speedy index queries. The API provides Spark applications with extensive relational/procedural interaction. DFs are collections of structured records that can be modified using either the procedural API of Spark or the new relational APIs that enable more efficient optimizations. They may be constructed directly from distributed Java/Python object collections, allowing relational processing in current Spark applications.

In this work, we utilize Spark SQL along with MongoDB to efficiently perform complex queries and improve their runtime. We investigate query optimization using various query execution paths by combining MongoDB and Spark SQL, aiming to minimize the average query execution time. We improve the query execution time by splitting the query into sub-queries, considering various scenarios that split sub-queries between MongoDB and Spark SQL, along with the use of the connector between Apache Spark and MongoDB. This mediator transfers either the entire database from MongoDB to Spark, or transfers a subset of the results for those sub-queries executed in MongoDB. Our experimental results with eight different query execution path scenarios and six difference database sizes (ranging from 500,000 to 20,000,000 records) demonstrate the clear superiority and scalability of a specific scenario.

The remainder of the paper is organized as follows. In Sect. 2 the fundamental elements of Spark, Resilient Distributed Datasets (RDDs), and MongoDB are presented. Section 3 describes the implementation of several query execution plans in MongoDB and Spark. Section 4 highlights the experimental results and their findings. Section 5 discusses the idea of sharding for further improvements on the query performance over huge data sets. Finally, conclusions and future directions of this work are presented in Sect. 6.

2 Preliminaries

Big Data refers to the deluge of digital data from a variety of digital sources, including sensors, scanners, smartphones, videos, e-mails, and social media. These data include texts, photos, videos, and sounds, as well as their combinations. In the big data era, applications require a combination of processing algorithms, data sources, and storage formats to accomplish a common goal which is big data processing. Nowadays this has turned toward big data warehouses [32] and high-performance computing environments that can handle geospatial

big data [21] among others. The initial systems built for these types of work-
loads, such as MapReduce which is offered by Apache Spark, provide users with
a strong yet procedural programming interface. However, such systems are difficult to program and need manual tuning by the user to get optimal performance.
As a consequence, a number of innovative technologies aimed to deliver a more
productive user experience by providing relational interfaces to large amounts of
data. Systems like Asterix, Hive, Dremel, and Shark [9,26,31,33] all use declarative queries to deliver more robust automated optimizations.

Apache Spark which is utilized in this work is a distributed cluster computing
engine with APIs in Scala, Java, and Python and libraries for streaming, graph
processing, and machine learning [28]. It is one of the most widely-used systems
with a language-integrated API similar to DryadLINQ [18], and the most active
open-source project for big data processing. Spark offers a functional programming API similar to other systems [11,18], where users manipulate distributed
collections called Resilient Distributed Datasets (RDDs) [34]. Each RDD is a set
of Java or Python objects partitioned throughout a cluster. RDDs can handle
operations like map, filter, and reduce, which take functions in the programming language and transfer them to nodes on the cluster. An example of a Scala
code that counts lines starting with "ERROR" within a text file is given below
(Listing 1):

Listing 1: Scala Example Code

```scala
lines = spark.textFile ("_hdfs_://...")
errors = lines.filter(s => s. contains ("_ERROR_"))
println(errors.count ())
```

The preceding example constructs an RDD of strings named lines by reading
an HDFS file, which then transforms it using a filter to obtain another RDD,
named errors, and then performs a count on this data. RDDs are fault toler-
ant meaning that the system can recover lost data using the lineage graph of
the RDDs by rerunning operations such as the filter above to rebuild missing
partitions. They can also explicitly be cached in memory or on disk to support
iteration [34]. One final note about the API is that RDDs are evaluated lazily.
Each RDD represents a "logical plan" to compute a dataset, but Spark waits
until certain output operations, to launch a function. This allows the engine to
perform some simple query optimization, such as pipelining operations.

In particular, Spark will pipeline reading lines from the HDFS file by applying
the filter and computing a running count, so that it never needs to materialize the
intermediate lines and error results. Although such optimizations are extremely
useful, they are also limited because the engine does not understand the structure of the data in RDDs which are Java/Python objects or the semantics of
user functions that contain arbitrary code. Nonetheless, the most basic data processing paradigms are relational queries that RDDs cannot manage. To address
this, Apache Spark requires a number of higher-level libraries. Spark SQL is one

of the innovative components of the Apache Spark Framework that combines relational processing with the functional programming API of Apache Spark. It enables Apache Spark developers to use the advantages of relational processing.

Spark SQL allows a seamless mix of SQL Queries within the environment of Apache Spark. Spark SQL is capable to perform data processing on structured data, or on Resource Description Framework (RDFs) stores, or in DataFrames (DFs). RDF is a graph-based data model, composed of triples (s, p, o); such a triple denotes a directed arc (s, o) with label p. RDFs can be applied to matrix computations [13] as well as to knowledge graph representations [2]. Spark SQL can support batch processing [3] of RDFs in a matter of seconds. It can also support storage, partitioning, indexing, and information retrieval in the spectrum of Big Data [12]. A DF is a distributed collection of data organized into named columns. Users can use a DataFrame API to perform various relational operations on both external data sources and Spark's built-in distributed collections without providing specific procedures for processing data.

Transiting from traditional SQL-based approaches to NoSQL techniques requires layers that convert relational databases to key-value stores. Numerous studies have suggested alternative layers to convert relational databases to NoSQL; however, the majority of them focused on just one or two models of NoSQL and assessed their layers on a single node, not in a distributed environment. Therefore, Spark-based layers that are able to map relational databases to NoSQL storage have emerged [1]. Of course, the necessity here is to utilize a connector that takes advantage of both distributed computing engines such as Spark and the exceptional speed that MongoDB has to offer as per searches in documents.

MongoDB [27] is a document-based NoSQL datastore that is commercially maintained by 10gen. MongoDB in particular is among the most promising databases existing because of its nature and its superior performance. Despite being a non-relational database, MongoDB provides several relational database functions, such as sorting, secondary indexing, range queries, and nested document querying. Operators like create, insert, read, update and remove as well as manual indexing, indexing on embedded documents and indexing on location-based data are also supported. In such systems, data are kept in documents, which are entities that offer structure and encoding for the managed data. Each page is effectively an associative array containing a scalar value, lists, or arrays nested inside arrays. Every document has a unique special key called "ObjectId" that is used for explicit identification, but this key and the document it corresponds to are conceptually comparable to a key-value pair.

Documents in MongoDB are serialised as Javascript Object Notation (JSON) objects and saved using a binary encoding of JSON known as BSON. MongoDB, like other NoSQL systems, has no schema limits and can allow semi-structured data, as well as multi-attribute lookups on records that may contain multiple types of key-value pairings [22]. Documents are often semi-structured files such as XML, JSON, YALM, and CSV. There are two methods for storing data: a) nesting documents inside each other, which may accommodate one-to-one or many-to-many relationships, and b) reference to documents, in which the referred document is only obtained when the user requests data from this document.

Cloud computing can be integrated with MongoDB databases along with modern technologies such as the Internet of Things (IoT) for streaming applications [16], or for IoT Data Management on the Cloud [15]. Cloud-based applications that promote and support smart cities and overall well-being in societies can enhance information management as a service [10].

3   Query Execution Plans

3.1   Indexing in MongoDB

Having previously discussed the use of Apache Spark and Spark SQL, we shall now provide a simple example of constructing an index and demonstrate how it influences the query runtime. For this purpose, we shall use the following example (Listing 2) of a MongoDB database, consisting of one million records.

Listing 2: Index Construction in MongoDB

```
{
    "_id":{"$oid":"61a6540c3838fe02b81e5338"},
    "Region":"Sub-Saharan_Africa",
    "Country":"South_Africa",
    "Item_Type":"Fruits",
    "Sales_Channel":"Offline",
    "Order_Priority":"M",
    "Order_Date":{"$date":"2012-07-26T21:00:00.000Z"},
    "Order_ID":443368995,
    "Ship_Date":{"$date":"2012-07-27T21:00:00.000Z"},
    "Units_Sold":1593,
    "Unit_Price":9.33,
    "Unit_Cost":6.92,
    "Total_Revenue":14862.69,
    "Total_Cost":11023.56,
    "Total_Profit":3839.13
}
```

Instead of storing the data in the form of tables with columns and rows, the data is stored as documents. Each document can be one of the relational matrices of the numerical values, or the overlapping interrelated arrays or matrices. These documents are serialized as JSON objects and stored internally using JSON binary encryption known as BSON in MongoDB. The data is partitioned and stored on several servers called shard servers for simultaneous access and effective read/write operations.

Assume that the following SQL query (Listing 3) is to be executed within the given database.

Listing 3: SQL Query

```
SELECT Country, Region, Unit Price, Unit Cost
    FROM sales
    WHERE Unit Price > 600
    AND Unit Cost < 510
    ORDER BY Region
```

The aforementioned query is well formatted in SQL, making it easy to comprehend. In order to execute the query in MongoDB, we make use of mongosh, a component of the MongoDB Compass tool[1] to construct the database.

The previous query can now be executed utilizing an equivalent function (Listing 4):

Listing 4: MongoDB Aggregation Function

```
db.myBigCollection.aggregate([{$project: {
    Country: 1, Region: 1, 'Unit_Price': 1,
    'Unit_Cost': 1}},
    {$match: {'Unit_Price': {$gt: 600},
    'Unit_Cost': {$lt: 510}}},
    {$sort: {Region: 1}}])
    .explain()
```

By utilizing the *explain()* function, we observed an average query execution time of 860 milliseconds (ms) for the specific database.

To improve the execution time of a certain query by creating an index, it is reasonable to believe that this index should be based on the columns "Unit Price" and "Unit Cost" on which the majority of the searches is performed.

Utilizing the following command (Listing 5), one compound index for the "Unit Price" and "Unit Cost" values are constructed in ascending order:

Listing 5: MongoDB Index Construction

```
db.myBigCollection.createIndex({"Unit_Price": 1,
"Unit_Cost": 1})
```

Now, the preceding query is re-executed and measured in terms of time. The execution time has been drastically lowered, varying from 250 to 270 ms. An

---

[1] Available at: https://www.mongodb.com/products/compass.

additional single-field index, depending on the field that is being used to sort the data, may be established. The following command (Listing 6) constructs a new index based on the "Region" field:

Listing 6: MongoDB New Index Construction

```
db.myBigCollection.createIndex({"Region": 1})
```

If the same query is re-executed utilising both indexes constructed, the average query execution time drops further to 220 ms. This demonstrates the significance of indexes, since the average execution time of a very basic query was lowered to roughly one fourth with the proper use of indexes.

3.2 Integration of MongoDB and Apache Spark

In this subsection, the information about MongoDB is applied to examine various instances of the MongoDB-Spark integration described in the previous Section. We will determine how to use the connection and how to apply our indexing methods, using the database and indexes described previously.

To highlight the differences among Spark SQL and MongoDB in terms of query execution, different operations must be considered. In general, MongoDB tends to be quicker for INSERT/UPDATE operations [17], while SQL appears to be faster for SELECT operations, but this is not a general rule. To investigate this problem, an identical database using DataFrames is constructed in Spark. We will execute the query from Sect. 3, and monitor its execution time.

Recall that without indexing, it took MongoDB an average of 860 ms to perform the query. Spark SQL executes the identical query in 310 ms without indexing, which is much faster than MongoDB. This already is a significant improvement in terms of time. The main reason that the execution time can be further improved in Spark SQL using indexing is that Apache Spark does not necessarily allow indexing in the same way as SQL does. Apache Spark is compatible with a range of data storage formats, some of which enable indexing while others do not. For instance, Spark along with PostgreSQL enables the usage of PostgreSQL indexes.

Having observed that Spark SQL executes certain queries faster than MongoDB, it becomes pretty clear that it is better to utilise a URL to get the data, rather than recreating a database in Apache Spark. Initially, Apache Spark is executed, including the link package named MongoDB Connector for Spark[2]. The initial objective here is to access the database generated previously in MongoDB and to transfer it to Spark. Using the following command (Listing 7), the data is transferred into a DataFrame, denoted by df.

---

[2] Available at: https://www.mongodb.com/docs/spark-connector/current/.

Listing 7: Dataframe Creation from MongoDB to Apache Spark

```
val df = spark.sqlContext.read.format
("com.mongodb.spark.sql.DefaultSource")
.option("uri",
"mongodb://127.0.0.1/myDb.myBigCollection")
.load()
```

Once the data are imported, a temporary SQL view of the "sales" DataFrame can be constructed utilizing the following command (Listing 8).

Listing 8: Temporary SQL View

```
df.createOrReplaceTempView("sales")
```

At this point, Spark SQL can be utilized to execute numerous queries on the database. We execute the query from Sect. 3 and measure its execution time for evaluation. To execute and measure the execution time of the query, the spark.sql() and spark.time() methods are used respectively as follows (Listing 9).

Listing 9: Spark SQL Query Time Measurement Command

```
spark.time(spark.sql(
SELECT Region, Country, 'Unit Price', 'Unit Cost'
    FROM sales
    WHERE 'Unit Price' > 600 AND 'Unit Cost' < 510
    ORDER BY Region).show())
```

The average execution time of the aforementioned query is 580 ms, which is much slower than the 220 ms of MongoDB. This is due to the fact that the connection transfers data in real-time, resulting in a significant increase in the average execution time required to move data from MongoDB to Spark. In particular, the entire database is transferred from MongoDB to Spark, while the query is executed, and the results are derived at the end.

Therefore, we should consider how we might save time by moving the database so that the query execution times are not that lengthy. One way to improve the query time is to execute the query on MongoDB and transfer only the results to Spark. That is, instead of transferring the entire database in the DataFrame, the portion of the database is simply transferred that pertains to the given query. This is done by utilizing the following commands (Listing 10).

Listing 10: MongoDB Query Execution and Transferring the Results to Spark

```
val df = spark.sqlContext.read.format
("com.mongodb.spark.sql.DefaultSource")
.option("uri",
"mongodb://127.0.0.1/myDb.myBigCollection")
.option("pipeline",
{$project: {Country: 1, Region: 1,
'Unit_Price': 1, 'Unit_Cost': 1}},
{$match: {'Unit_Price': {$gt: 600 },
'Unit_Cost': {$lt: 510}}}, {$sort: {Region: 1}}).load()
```

Once the necessary information in the DataFrame exists, the results can be examined. After creating a temporary SQL view of the DataFrame with the same name "sales" (for convenience), a single query is executed to return all fields, as the DataFrame includes the required information. This is done through the following query (Listing 11):

Listing 11: Spark SQL Query Execution

```
spark.time(spark.sql(SELECT * FROM sales).show())
```

As anticipated, the average query execution time now drops to 180 ms. This time is lower than that of the MongoDB (220 ms) and this is due to the following reasons.

Recall first the two query scenarios. In the first scenario, the query is executed in MongoDB and the results are reported in MongoDB. In the second scenario, the query is executed in MongoDB, the data are transferred to Spark, and then the results are reported there. The obvious question is how the query execution time of the second scenario turns out to be faster than that of the first scenario, given the fact that the second scenario (and its corresponding execution path) requires more time due to the transfer of data.

The reason appears to be in the speed at which the query is executed using a SELECT operation in Spark SQL against the operations of MongoDB, as previously noted. Performing more experiments in the whole database in both MongoDB and Spark SQL (after transferring it), it appears that Spark SQL performs the SELECT operation significantly faster. In the second scenario, the complete database transfer is not required, but only a tiny portion of it that contains the results which are sent after the queries. Hence, the overall execution time will be much less. In the particular example used, around 83,000 records are returned out of the total of one million records in the database.

A subsequent question is whether the query execution time can be further reduced by exploiting the speed of the SELECT(Spark SQL) operation against that of the $project(MongoDB) operation. To investigate this idea, we divide the query into sub-queries. In particular, we split the query so that the WHERE($match) and the ORDER BY($sort) operations are executed in MongoDB, while the operation SELECT($project) is executed on Spark.

To execute the operations WHERE($match) and ORDER BY($sort) in MongoDB the following commands (Listing 12) are used.

Listing 12: MongoDB WHERE and ORDER BY Query Execution

```
val df = spark.sqlContext.read.format
("com.mongodb.spark.sql.DefaultSource")
.option("uri",
"mongodb://127.0.0.1/myDb.myBigCollection")
.option("pipeline", {$match: {'Unit_Price': {$gt: 600},
'Unit_Cost': {$lt: 510}}}, {$sort: {Region: 1}}).load()
```

To execute the operation SELECT($project) in SparkSQL the following commands (Listing 13) are used.

Listing 13: Spark SQL SELECT Command Execution

```
spark.time(spark.sql(SELECT Region, Country,
'Unit Price', 'Unit Cost' FROM sales).show())
```

Measuring now the average query execution time, we observe that it has been further reduced to approximately 105 ms. Spark SQL appears to be faster than MongoDB when executing the operation SELECT from $project.

Based on this additional improvement, a natural attempt would be to migrate the ORDER BY($sort) portion of the query to Spark SQL. This is done in two steps.

First, the operation WHERE($match) is executed in MongoDB using the following commands (Listing 14).

Listing 14: MongoDB WHERE Command Execution

```
val df = spark.sqlContext.read.format
("com.mongodb.spark.sql.DefaultSource")
.option("uri",
"mongodb://127.0.0.1/myDb.myBigCollection")
.option("pipeline", {$match: {'Unit_Price':
{$gt: 600}, 'Unit_Cost': {$lt: 510}}})
.load()
```

Then, the operations SELECT($project) and ORDER BY($sort) are executed in Spark SQL using the following commands (Listing 15).

Listing 15: Spark SQL SELECT and ORDER BY Execution

```
spark.time(spark.sql(SELECT Region, Country,
'Unit Price', 'Unit Cost' FROM sales ORDER BY
Region).show())
```

Measuring the query execution time of this experiment, we observed that the average time did not improve but rather increased significantly to 530 ms. This implies that the ORDER BY($sort) method in MongoDB appears to be sufficiently faster.

The discussion in this section demonstrates the need to consider various query execution scenarios and measuring the corresponding query execution times in order to recommend some best cases/practices. We do this in Sect. 4 where various scenarios are analysed and their query execution times are reported.

4   Experimental Results

In this Section we present the experimental results by running various scenarios of query execution paths on different database sizes and measure the average query execution time.

We considered the eight query execution path scenarios shown in Table 1, in which one part of the query is executed in MongoDB and the other part in Spark SQL (examples of such query scenarios were presented in Sect. 3.

The aforementioned scenarios were executed on six different database sizes in order to investigate the scalability of the specific query execution scenarios.

We initiated the database size to 500,000 records and doubled the size for generating the next database instance up to 20,000,000 records.

The average query times per scenario and database size are reported in Tables 2 to 7. The fastest query times are highlighted in bold.

We observe the following across all results (cf. Tables 2 to 7).

Table 1. Scenarios of Query Execution Paths.

Scenario	MongoDB	Spark SQL
1	Entire Query Execution	–
2	Entire Database Transfer	Entire Query Execution
3	WHERE($match) + ORDER BY($sort)	SELECT($project)
4	WHERE($match)	SELECT($project) + ORDER BY($sort)
5	ORDER BY($sort)	SELECT($project) + WHERE($match)
6	SELECT($project)	WHERE($match) + ORDER BY($sort)
7	SELECT($project) + WHERE ($match)	ORDER BY($sort)
8	SELECT($project) + ORDER BY($sort)	WHERE($match)

Table 2. Average query execution time (in ms) per scenario for 500,000 records.

Scenario	MongoDB	Spark SQL	Avg Qtime (ms)
1	Entire Query Execution	–	121
2	Entire Database Transfer	Entire Query Execution	311
3	WHERE($match) + ORDER BY($sort)	SELECT($project)	72
4	WHERE($match)	SELECT($project) + ORDER BY($sort)	289
5	ORDER BY($sort)	SELECT($project) + WHERE($match)	**48**
6	SELECT($project)	WHERE($match) + ORDER BY($sort)	672
7	SELECT($project) + WHERE ($match)	ORDER BY($sort)	518
8	SELECT($project) + ORDER BY($sort)	WHERE($match)	127

Table 3. Average query execution time (in ms) per scenario for 1,000,000 records.

Scenario	MongoDB	Spark SQL	Avg Qtime (ms)
1	Entire Query Execution	–	180
2	Entire Database Transfer	Entire Query Execution	580
3	WHERE($match) + ORDER BY($sort)	SELECT($project)	105
4	WHERE($match)	SELECT($project) + ORDER BY($sort)	530
5	ORDER BY($sort)	SELECT($project) + WHERE($match)	**55**
6	SELECT($project)	WHERE($match) + ORDER BY($sort)	850
7	SELECT($project) + WHERE ($match)	ORDER BY($sort)	690
8	SELECT($project) + ORDER BY($sort)	WHERE($match)	210

Table 4. Average query execution time (in ms) per scenario for 2,000,000 records.

Scenario	MongoDB	Spark SQL	Avg Qtime (ms)
1	Entire Query Execution	–	337
2	Entire Database Transfer	Entire Query Execution	1429
3	WHERE($match) + ORDER BY($sort)	SELECT($project)	184
4	WHERE($match)	SELECT($project) + ORDER BY($sort)	1185
5	ORDER BY($sort)	SELECT($project) + WHERE($match)	**59**
6	SELECT($project)	WHERE($match) + ORDER BY($sort)	1338
7	SELECT($project) + WHERE ($match)	ORDER BY($sort)	1129
8	SELECT($project) + ORDER BY($sort)	WHERE($match)	369

Table 5. Average query execution time (in ms) per scenario for 5,000,000 records.

Scenario	MongoDB	Spark SQL	Avg Qtime (ms)
1	Entire Query Execution	–	670
2	Entire Database Transfer	Entire Query Execution	8800
3	WHERE($match) + ORDER BY($sort)	SELECT($project)	1270
4	WHERE($match) + SELECT($project)	ORDER BY($sort)	6300
5	ORDER BY($sort)	SELECT($project) + WHERE($match)	**65**
6	SELECT($project)	WHERE($match) + ORDER BY($sort)	3048
7	SELECT($project) + WHERE ($match)	ORDER BY($sort)	2438
8	SELECT($project) + ORDER BY($sort)	WHERE($match)	844

Table 6. Average query execution time (in ms) per scenario for 10,000,000 records.

Scenario	MongoDB	Spark SQL	Avg Qtime (ms)
1	Entire Query Execution	–	1237
2	Entire Database Transfer	Entire Query Execution	11469
3	WHERE($match) + ORDER BY($sort)	SELECT($project)	2543
4	WHERE($match) + SELECT($project)	ORDER BY($sort)	12894
5	ORDER BY($sort)	SELECT($project) + WHERE($match)	**102**
6	SELECT($project)	WHERE($match) + ORDER BY($sort)	5671
7	SELECT($project) + WHERE ($match)	ORDER BY($sort)	4179
8	SELECT($project) + ORDER BY($sort)	WHERE($match)	1636

Table 7. Average query execution time (in ms) per scenario for 20,000,000 records.

Scenario	MongoDB	Spark SQL	Avg Qtime (ms)
1	Entire Query Execution	–	3659
2	Entire Database Transfer	Entire Query Execution	Out of memory
3	WHERE($match) + ORDER BY($sort)	SELECT($project)	6784
4	WHERE($match) + SELECT($project)	ORDER BY($sort)	Out of memory
5	ORDER BY($sort)	SELECT($project) + WHERE($match)	**285**
6	SELECT($project)	WHERE($match) + ORDER BY($sort)	11074
7	SELECT($project) + WHERE ($match)	ORDER BY($sort)	8514
8	SELECT($project) + ORDER BY($sort)	WHERE($match)	4855

The ORDER BY($sort) operation in MongoDB is exceptionally fast, faster than any other operation.

The SELECT($project) operation in Spark SQL is faster compared to the same operation in MongoDB.

The combination of the SELECT($project) and WHERE($match) operations in Spark SQL are exceptionally fast, faster than any other operation.

Scenario 5 is the fastest across all database sizes, due to the above facts.

Scenario 3 is the second fastest scenario for database sizes up to 2,000,000 records, followed by scenarios 1 and 8 (cf. Tables 2 to 4).

As soon as the database size exceeds 2,000,000 records (cf. Tables 5 to 7), the transfer of a large amount of data between MongoDB and Spark begins to have a significant effect on the query execution time. This is also evident by the query execution time of scenario 2, in which the entire database is transferred to Sparl SQL, and which has the largest value, while the memory exceeded its limit in the case of the database with 20,000,000 records (cf. Table 7).

For database sizes beyond 2,000,000 records, scenario 1 (i.e., just run the entire query in MongoDB) is the second fastest, followed by scenarios 8 and 3 (cf. Tables 5 to 7).

Scenario 5 has an exceptional scalability not only because it is the fastest across all database sizes, but also due to the very good scaling of the average query execution time as the size of the database doubles from one instance to the next (cf. Tables 2 to 7).

The log-scaled results across all 8 different test scenarios and the 6 different database sizes are shown in Figs. 1 and 2.

Figure 1 presents the results across all databases sizes for scenarios 1–4. As we can see, scenarios 1 and 2 have similar behavior across all database sizes. The only difference appears in the case of scenario 2 and database size of 20,000,000 records, where the memory exceeded its limits. Scenario 3 remains the fastest execution plan across all database sizes, while we see an increase in time at 20,000,000 records. Lastly, scenario 4 has similar performance to scenario 2, but once again when the size of the database reaches 20,000,000 records the memory exceeded its limits.

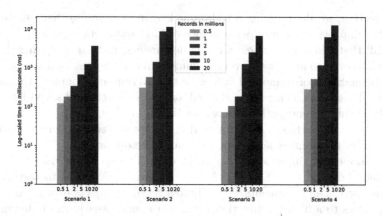

Fig. 1. Query Runtime for Scenarios 1-4 for 0.5, 1, 2, 5, 10 and 20 million records.

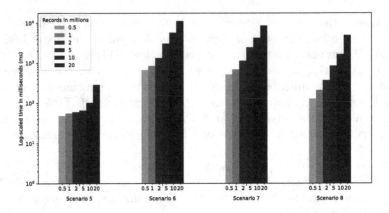

Fig. 2. Query Runtime for Scenarios 5-8 for 0.5, 1, 2, 5, 10 and 20 million records.

Figure 2 presents the results across all databases sizes for scenarios 5–8. As we can see, scenario 5 is the fastest as per query execution time across all database sizes. Scenario 6 appears to be the slowest. Scenario 8 is the second best. Both scenarios 7 and 8 have similar behavior across all database sizes. We also observed that scenarios 5–8 did not cause the memory to reach its limits.

5   Further Extensions

In this section, we shall discuss a technique known as *sharding* that can be used to further improve the query performance of huge data sets.

Recall that MongoDB stores data as documents, instead of storing data as tables with columns and rows. Every document may be represented by one of the relational matrices of numerical values or the overlapping connected arrays or matrices. These documents are serialised as JSON objects and saved internally using JSON binary encryption (known as BSON in MongoDB).

The data are partitioned and stored on many servers known as *shards* or *shard servers* to facilitate simultaneous read/write operations.

This connection integrates MongoDB with Apache Spark using a cluster assignment function $C : X \rightarrow \{1, 2, \ldots, K\}$, where K refers to the number of clusters across all documents, X refers to a set of N objects (documents), and $d \in \mathbb{R}_0^+$ refers to a distance function (symmetric, non-negative and obeying the triangle inequality) between all pairs of objects in X.

Then, the goal is to partition X into K disjoint sets

$$X_1, X_2, \ldots, X_K$$

such that $\sum_{x,x' \in X_p} d(x, x')$ is minimized for each $1 \leq p \leq K$, while the distance $d(y, y')$ between any two points $y \in X_i$ and $y' \in X_j$, $i \neq j$, is maximized.

The number of all possible distinct cluster assignments $S(N, K)$ is given by

$$S(N, K) = \frac{1}{K!} \sum_{p=1}^{K} (-1)^{K-p} \binom{K}{p} p^N \qquad (1)$$

The function $S(N, K)$ can be used to determine the optimal cluster assignment function C for a given set of data, by finding the value of p that minimizes the value of $S(N, K)$. In the context of sharding, this could be used to find the optimal number of shards (corresponding to clusters) for a database or any other distributed system by minimizing the number of shards needed to store a given amount of data.

Sharding is a way to distribute data across multiple devices, to deal with applications that use huge databases and structures. A database may have a mix of sharded collections and unsharded collections.

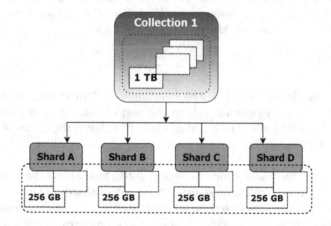

Fig. 3. Sharding Phase of MongoDB

Sharding in MongoDB uses subsets of data which are later moved from one shard to another; cf. Fig. 3. One way to identify which subset is being moved is by the selected key. For example, if we were to split a collection of users based on the field username, then the data is split into *chunks* (parts of a file) of predefined ranges e.g., ["a","f")[3]. Then "a", "charlie", and "ezbake" could be in the set, but "f" could not.

A MongoDB shard cluster is comprised of two or more shards, one or more configuration servers, and an arbitrary number of routing processes. Each component is detailed below.

---

[3] The standard range notation is used where "[" and "]" denote inclusive bounds and "(" and ")" denote exclusive bounds.

- *Shard*: each shard consists of one or more servers and uses MongoDB processes to store data. Each shard in a production environment will consist of a replica set to ensure availability and automated fail-over.
- *Configuration server*: it stores the metadata of the cluster, which includes basic information about each shard server and the chunks it contains.
- *Mongos (Routing Processes)*: they concernt the routing and coordination processes. When MongoDB receives a request from a client, it routes the request to the appropriate server and merges the results before sending them back to the client.

Sharded sets are divided into clusters and spread throughout the shards, using a cluster assignment function, as discussed above. Unsharded collections are stored on the main shard.

MongoDB measures the theoretical maximum collection size as follows. Let B_{max} be the maximum BSON document size (in MB) and let Y_{avg} be the average size of shard key values (in bytes). Then, the maximum number M of splits is given by $M = B_{max}/Y_{avg}$. Assuming a chunk size of H (in MB), we have that the maximum collection size M_B (in MB) is given by

$$M_B = \frac{M \cdot C}{2} \tag{2}$$

The size of the chunks, which is the basic unit of data movement in sharded clusters, also plays a significant role in the performance of operations such as migrations. Adjusting the chunk size can help to balance the trade-offs between the need for data movement and the need to keep chunks small enough to prevent hotspots[4].

An additional technique concerns *zone sharding* that allows the assignment of ranges of shard keys to different shards, or a group of shards. This technique can be used to distribute data based on access patterns; for instance, assigning frequently accessed data to a specific set of shards can improve query performance. Furthermore, complex queries can be split and executed on specific shards based on their complexity and the capacity of the selected shard.

In order to achieve optimal performance in MongoDB, it is essential to constantly monitor and optimize the sharding configuration by considering the usage of sharding in the query execution plan, monitoring and optimizing the sharding configuration, choosing the right shard key, indexes, chunk size, and using techniques like zone sharding. These steps can greatly improve the performance of MongoDB in a large and complex data environment.

6 Conclusions and Future Work

We presented an approach for query optimization in terms of average query execution time for NoSQL databases and Spark SQL. The query execution path

---

[4] Hotspots in sharded clusters refer to situations where a specific chunk of data receives a disproportionate amount of read and write operations, causing performance issues.

scenarios that were examined demonstrate that our results are promising. By examining the aforementioned database instances and scenarios, the objective of this work was to determine how the connection among MongoDB and Apache Spark operates and therefore to investigate potential optimization possibilities using the connector and the indexing algorithms offered by MongoDB. One of our findings is that the SELECT operation in Spark SQL is typically faster compared to the same operation in MongoDB.

To further substantiate this finding, one could investigate as many potential scenarios as possible, in order to either discover the optimal answer to a given question, or to detect optimization tendencies. Naturally, the integration of all conceivable scenarios and conditions is endless and therefore it is impossible to map all feasible improvements for each specific instance. This work can be considered as a useful step forward to SQL query optimization in distributed systems utilizing NoSQL databases. Based on our current approach, our outcomes and the evaluated methodologies, we also believe that this work can be further expanded.

Future directions include collaborating with major organisations, businesses, and cooperatives that can provide a portion of their vast amounts of real-world data, in order to develop a variety of optimization models based on the current work. Hence, it will be possible to detect broad optimization tendencies based on the used databases and the frequency of queries. Thus, the database administrators (used to establish their own database) will be able in the future to utilize these models and adjust their database and query path execution plans to them.

The preceding directions may be performed automatically by using a smart query optimizer as the ones presented in [8,19,20,23–25,29]. However, the implementation of such a tool should combine query evaluation and optimization methods along with machine learning techniques. We strongly believe that these methods would be interesting to be used on specific use cases, where after several experiments the appropriate cost functions can be found in order to create one highly efficient query execution scheduler able to scale and adapt.

To further improve the query execution time, one approach is to distribute a given complex query to sharded queries on RDDs (cf. Sect. 5) based on the operations contained within it so as to improve the time, and then to collect the sub-results from RDDs and merge them to construct the answer to the initial query. Ultimately, a fine-tuning direction would be to utilize modified indexes such as R-trees, Quad-trees, kD-trees and LSM-trees, which have been already implemented, for integration with this work rather than using the MongoDB B-tree index.

References

1. Abdel-Fattah, M.A., Mohamed, W., Abdelgaber, S.: A comprehensive spark-based layer for converting relational databases to NoSQL. Big Data Cogn. Comput. **6**(3), 71 (2022). https://doi.org/10.3390/bdcc6030071
2. Ali, W., Saleem, M., Yao, B., Hogan, A., Ngomo, A.-C.N.: A survey of RDF stores & SPARQL engines for querying knowledge graphs. VLDB J. **31**, 1–26 (2021). https://doi.org/10.1007/s00778-021-00711-3

3. Anusha, K., Usha Rani, K.: Performance evaluation of spark SQL for batch processing. In: Venkata Krishna, P., Obaidat, M.S. (eds.) Emerging Research in Data Engineering Systems and Computer Communications. AISC, vol. 1054, pp. 145–153. Springer, Singapore (2020). https://doi.org/10.1007/978-981-15-0135-7_13
4. Apache: Hadoop. https://hadoop.apache.org/. Accessed 17 Jan 2023
5. Apache: HBase. http://hbase.apache.org/. Accessed 17 Jan 2023
6. Apache: Spark. https://spark.apache.org/. Accessed 17 Jan 2023
7. Apache: Storm. https://storm.apache.org/. Accessed 17 Jan 2023
8. Babcock, B., Chaudhuri, S.: Towards a robust query optimizer: a principled and practical approach. In: Proceedings of the 2005 ACM SIGMOD International Conference on Management of Data, pp. 119–130 (2005)
9. Behm, A., Behm, A., et al.: ASTERIX: towards a scalable, semistructured data platform for evolving-world models. Distrib. Parall. Databases **29**(3), 185–216 (2011)
10. Celesti, A., et al.: Information management in IoT cloud-based tele-rehabilitation as a service for smart cities: Comparison of NoSQL approaches. Measurement **151**, 107218 (2020). https://doi.org/10.1016/j.measurement.2019.107218
11. Chambers, C., et al.: Flumejava: easy, efficient data-parallel pipelines. ACM SIGPLAN Notices **45**(6), 363–375 (2010)
12. Chawla, T., Singh, G., Pilli, E.S., Govil, M.: Storage, partitioning, indexing and retrieval in big RDF frameworks: a survey. Comput. Sci. Rev. **38**, 100309 (2020). https://doi.org/10.1016/j.cosrev.2020.100309
13. Chen, Y., Özsu, M.T., Xiao, G., Tang, Z., Li, K.: GSmart: an efficient SPARQL query engine using sparse matrix algebra - full version. arXiv preprint arXiv:2106.14038 (2021)
14. Dean, J., Ghemawat, S.: MapReduce: Simplified Data Processing on Large Clusters. Commun. ACM **51**(1), 107–113 (2008). https://doi.org/10.1145/1327452.1327492
15. Eyada, M.M., Saber, W., El Genidy, M.M., Amer, F.: Performance evaluation of IoT data management using MongoDB versus MySQL databases in different cloud environments. IEEE Access **8**, 110656–110668 (2020). https://doi.org/10.1109/ACCESS.2020.3002164
16. Gupta, A., Jain, S.: Optimizing performance of real-time big data stateful streaming applications on cloud. In: 2022 IEEE International Conference on Big Data and Smart Computing (BigComp), pp. 1–4 (2022). https://doi.org/10.1109/BigComp54360.2022.00010
17. Győrödi, C., Győrödi, R., Pecherle, G., Olah, A.: A comparative study: MongoDB vs. MySQL. In: 2015 13th International Conference on Engineering of Modern Electric Systems (EMES), pp. 1–6. IEEE (2015)
18. Isard, M., Yu, Y.: Distributed data-parallel computing using a high-level programming language. In: Proceedings of the 2009 ACM SIGMOD International Conference on Management of Data, pp. 987–994 (2009)
19. Izenov, Y., Datta, A., Rusu, F., Shin, J.H.: COMPASS: Online sketch-based query optimization for in-memory databases. In: Proceedings of the 2021 International Conference on Management of Data, pp. 804–816 (2021)
20. Karras, A., Karras, C., Samoladas, D., Giotopoulos, K.C., Sioutas, S.: Query optimization in NoSQL databases using an enhanced localized R-tree index. In: Pardede, E., Delir Haghighi, P., Khalil, I., Kotsis, G. (eds.) Information Integration and Web Intelligence, pp. 391–398. Springer Nature Switzerland, Cham (2022)

21. Li, Z.: Geospatial big data handling with high performance computing: current approaches and future directions. In: Tang, W., Wang, S. (eds.) High Performance Computing for Geospatial Applications. GE, vol. 23, pp. 53–76. Springer, Cham (2020). https://doi.org/10.1007/978-3-030-47998-5_4

22. Makris, A., Tserpes, K., Andronikou, V., Anagnostopoulos, D.: A classification of NoSQL data stores based on key design characteristics. Procedia Comput. Sci. **97**, 94–103 (2016). https://doi.org/10.1016/j.procs.2016.08.284, 2nd International Conference on Cloud Forward: From Distributed to Complete Computing

23. Marcus, R., Negi, P., Mao, H., Tatbul, N., Alizadeh, M., Kraska, T.: Bao: making learned query optimization practical. ACM SIGMOD Rec. **51**(1), 6–13 (2022)

24. Marcus, R., et al.: Neo: a Learned Query Optimizer. Proc. VLDB Endow. **12**(11), 1705–1718 (2019). https://doi.org/10.14778/3342263.3342644

25. Markl, V., Lohman, G.M., Raman, V.: LEO: An autonomic query optimizer for DB2. IBM Syst. J. **42**(1), 98–106 (2003)

26. Melnik, S., et al.: Dremel: interactive analysis of web-scale datasets. Proceed. VLDB Endow. **3**(1–2), 330–339 (2010)

27. MongoDB Inc.: MongoDB. https://www.mongodb.com/. Accessed 24 Dec 2022

28. Salloum, S., Dautov, R., Chen, X., Peng, P.X., Huang, J.Z.: Big data analytics on Apache Spark. Int. J. Data Sci. Anal. **1**(3), 145–164 (2016). https://doi.org/10.1007/s41060-016-0027-9

29. Sellami, R., Defude, B.: Complex queries optimization and evaluation over relational and NoSQL data stores in cloud environments. IEEE Trans. Big Data **4**(2), 217–230 (2017)

30. Shvachko, K., Kuang, H., Radia, S., Chansler, R.: The Hadoop distributed file system. In: 2010 IEEE 26th Symposium on Mass Storage Systems and Technologies (MSST), pp. 1–10. IEEE (2010)

31. Thusoo, A., et al.: Hive-a petabyte scale data warehouse using Hadoop. In: 2010 IEEE 26th International Conference on Data Engineering (ICDE 2010), pp. 996–1005. IEEE (2010)

32. Vaisman, A., Zimányi, E.: Recent Developments in Big Data Warehouses. In: Data Warehouse Systems. Data-Centric Systems and Applications, pp. 561–631. Springer, Heidelberg (2022). https://doi.org/10.1007/978-3-662-65167-4_15

33. Xin, R.S., Rosen, J., Zaharia, M., Franklin, M.J., Shenker, S., Stoica, I.: Shark: SQL and rich analytics at scale. In: Proceedings of the 2013 ACM SIGMOD International Conference on Management of Data, pp. 13–24 (2013)

34. Zaharia, M., et al.: Resilient distributed datasets: a fault-tolerant abstraction for in-memory cluster computing. In: 9th USENIX Symposium on Networked Systems Design and Implementation (NSDI 12), pp. 15–28 (2012)

MAGMA: Proposing a Massive Historical Graph Management System

Alexandros Spitalas$^{(\boxtimes)}$ and Kostas Tsichlas

University of Patras, Rion, Patra, Greece
`a.spitalas@upatras.gr`, `ktsichlas@ceid.upatras.gr`

Abstract. In recent years, maintaining the history of graphs has become more and more imperative due to the emergence of related applications in a number of fields like health services, social interactions, and map guidance. Historical graphs focus on being able to store and query the whole evolution of the graph and not just the latest instance. In this paper we have two goals: 1) provide a concise survey of the state-of-art with respect to systems in historical graph management since no such comprehensive discussion exists and 2) propose an architecture for a distributed historical graph management system (named MAGMA - MAssive Graph MAnagement) based on previous research work of the authors.

Keywords: temporal graphs · graph management systems · query engine

1 Introduction

In recent years there is a rapid increase of time-evolving networks that produce a considerable amount of data. Networks, such as citation networks, traffic networks, and social networks are, naturally represented as graphs and they are usually dynamic. For example, in a citation network, new nodes and edges are constantly added due to the publication of new papers. An important challenge that arises in these time-evolving networks is the efficient management of their history in order to be able to reason about its whole evolution and not only about its latest state. This allows us to answer queries such as "what is the average connectivity of author X in the citation network between 2010 and 2015".

There have been quite a lot of systems developed since 2016 for historical graph management. Most of them are distributed, since evolving large graphs an extremely demanding with respect to space usage and query/update time. A rather outdated (since 2016) related survey can be found in [41]. They focus mainly on the models used for temporal graphs and the techniques available to query them. Another recent survey is [2] (2021) which analyzes graph streaming

The research work was supported by the Hellenic Foundation for Research and Innovation (HFRI) under the HFRI PhD Fellowship grant.

L. Foschini and S. Kontogiannis (Eds.): ALGOCLOUD 2022, LNCS 13799, pp. 42–57, 2023.
https://doi.org/10.1007/978-3-031-33437-5_3

systems, where the differences and similarities between graph streaming systems and historical graph systems are explicitly given. In general, graph streaming systems tend to use snapshots as the stable (latest) instance of the graph, since it may be the case that recent updates have not been registered. However, in principle these snapshots may be stored and allow for historical queries as well. Some graph streaming systems explicitly - although it is controversial to what extent - support historical queries on such (small number) snapshots of their evolution.

Our contribution in this paper is twofold. First, we provide a concise but comprehensive discussion on the systems developed up to today after 2016 that is covered by the survey of [41]. Due to space limitations, we do not discuss extensively these systems. At the same time, we focus mainly on distributed systems making a simple reference to non-distributed ones. To the best of our knowledge, there is no other up-to-date comprehensive reference to such systems. Our second contribution, which required this state-of-the-art review, is the proposal of the high-level architecture of a distributed system for managing time-evolving graphs. The architecture is based on the ideas set by the authors in previous papers [22, 23, 38] as well as by the most recent developments in the area of historical graph management, as laid out in our small survey.

The rest of the paper is structured as follows. In Sect. 2 we provide a review of historical graph management systems after 2016. In Sect. 3 we discuss the high-level architecture of the system we intend to implement for managing historical graphs. Finally, we conclude in Sect. 4.

2   A Review of Historical Graph Management Systems

Historical graphs have to utilize multiple dimensions resulting in many possible directions for such a system. Most systems are concerned with the storage and query of the evolution of the attributes as time evolves and some try to utilize the evolution of the topology for better partitioning or for reasons related to efficiency. In Table 1, we provide, without further discussion, some basic characteristics of non-distributed historical graph management systems. Some terminology is in order to understand the following tables:

1. **transaction time vs valid time:** Transaction time represents the time that an event takes place (i.e. the moment that a node is stored or deleted from a network) whereas valid time signifies the time period in which an object was valid (i.e. the time interval that a node existed in a database). In the transaction time setting updates can only occur in an append-like manner (i.e. an update in a field changes the value of the most recently stored value) whereas in the valid time setting updates can refer to any time point.

2. **time as a property vs snapshots:** in a rather crude manner, we get basically two different representations of time-evolving networks: a) snapshots, which correspond to a copy+log method; that is, the network is stored at specific time instances and in between a log is kept with the changes and b)

time as a property, which correspond to incorporating the notion of time as another special property of the objects/properties within a network. There are many variations of these two basic representations.

3. **offline vs online vs streaming:** In an offline setting, we get all the history of the graph beforehand. In an online setting, the graph evolves and with it the database, while queries can be made at any time. In a streaming setting, we have an online setting with restrictions as to how much space and time is allowed for each update. In the literature, streaming is not usually related to historical information but more to computational restrictions on the processing of the stream due to its high velocity and massiveness. One can get as a by-product a rudimentary transaction time temporal graph processing system.

4. **Time-dependent and Time-independent algorithms:** If the algorithm on the temporal graph can be applied without time constraints then it is time-independent (e.g., pagerank computation at time instance t). If there are time constraints, then the algorithm is time-dependent (e.g., shortest path that respects time intervals on nodes/edges and the journey is time-consistent).

In Table 2 we show all distributed systems for historical graph management after the year 2016. Since our proposed system falls under this category we are going to discuss briefly some of these systems, which according to our opinion are quite important and have nice properties.

Table 1. Non-distributed systems for historical graph management.

Summarizing the Characteristics of Non-Distributed Temporal Graph Management Systems

Systems	Memory	Storage Model	Time-related characteristics
InteractionGraph [10]	Main Memory (old graph in disk)	Custom	Transaction time
STVG [28]	Main Memory	Neo4j	valid time, offline, restricted to transit networks
ASPEN [7]	In-Memory/parallel	extends Ligra	Streaming
GraphOne [24]	in-memory NVMe SSD	Custom	Streaming, can't get arbitrary historic views if transaction time is assumed
Auxo [12]	Main and External Memory	Custom	Transaction time
[3]	Main Memory	Custom	Transaction time, Snapshot-based, focus on space savings
[1]	Main Memory	Neo4j	Valid time, In addition to entity evolution it supports schema evolution
TGraph [15]	Main and External Memory	Neo4j	Support ACID Transactions, slow topological updates but fast property updates, Transaction time
VersionTraveller [18]	Main Memory	based on PowerGraph static graph management system	Offline Snapshot-based, Focus on switching between snapshots
NVGraph [27]	Non-Volatile Main Memory and DRAM	Custom	Online Snapshot-based, Transaction time

Table 2. Distributed systems for historical graph management.

Summarizing the Characteristics of Distributed Temporal Graph Management Systems		
Systems	Storage Model	Time-related characteristics
Portal [33]	Spark	Offline, time as a property, Valid time
GDBAlive [29]	Cassandra	Transaction time
Graphsurge [37]	Custom	offline snapshots, focus on differential computation across multiple snapshots
TEGRA [17]	Custom	Transaction time, based on persistent trees, incremental computation model, window analytics
GraphTau [16]	Spark	Streaming
Immortalgraph [30]	Custom	Transaction time, Snapshot-based, Focus on locality-aware (w.r.t. time and topology by replication) batch scheduling for computation
HGS [21]	Cassandra	Transaction Time, Sophisticated Snapshot-based
SystemG-MV [40]	IBMs SystemG	Relaxed transaction time
Raphtory [39]	Custom + Cassandra for archiving	Transaction time, streaming
Chronograph [5]	MongoDB	offline, time as a property, Focus on graph traversals
Graphite [9]	Apache Giraph	offline, Time-dependent and time-independent algs
Granite [34]	Based on Graphite	focus on temporal path queries, partition techniques to keep everything in main memory
Tink [26]	Apache Flink	Online, Valid time
Gradoop - TPGM [6,35,36]	Apache HBase/ Accumulo	Valid and Transaction time (bitemporal), Fully-fledged system ranging from a graph analytical language to the storage model
Greycat [14]	NoSQL Database + custom	Valid time, No edge attributes
PAST [8]	based on key/value stores (e.g., Cassandra)	Streaming Spatio-temporal graphs, bipartite graphs, only edges with time-points, spatiotemporal-specific query workloads
HINODE [22,23,38]	Custom (other versions are based on Cassandra and MongoDB)	Online, time as a property, Valid time (allows more general notions of time), pure vertex-centric storage model

HINODE was the first pure vertex-centric system with respect to the storage model. It was introduced in [23] and supports valid time as well as extensions like multiple universes. It was implemented within the G^* system [25] by replacing its storage subsystem. They showed gains in space usage, which is an immediate consequence of the pure vertex-centric approach. They supported local queries (e.g., 2-hop queries) as well as global queries (e.g., clustering coefficient). In addition, this vertex-centric model was also adapted for NoSQL databases by creating two models, SingleTable (ST) and MultipleTable (MT). In the former, all data fit in one table and a row has the data of a Diachronic Node, while in the latter, data are split in different tables. Two implementations were made, one in Cassandra [22] and later one in MongoDB [38] for comparison reasons, while in MongoDB we tried also to take advantage of indexes and iterative computation to reduce memory usage.

Portal. In [33] they discuss about interval-based and point-based models preferring the interval-based model with sequenced semantics. As a data model, they talk about TGraph that uses the property graph model while they also discuss about sequenced semantics in a distributed environment (e.g. partitioning, time-window operations). In PhD Thesis [32] they propose a Temporal Graph Algebra (TGA) and a temporal graph model (TGraph) supporting TGA In addition, in [31] they propose a declarative language (Portal) based on the previous model and built on top of a distributed system (Apache Spark). Portal has SQL-like syntax following SQL:2011 standard. They also discuss about possible algorithms on temporal graphs among which are node influence over time, graph centrality over time, communities over time, and spread of information. TGraph is a valid time model that extends the property graph model (each edge and vertex is associated with a period of validity), while all relations in Graph must meet 5 criteria (uniqueness of vertices/edges, referential integrity, coalesced, required property, constant edge association). TGA is both snapshot and extended snapshot reducible presenting a new primitive (resolve) while containing operators like trim, map, and aggregation. Portal uses Spark for in-memory representation and processing while it uses Apache Parquet for on-disk data layout using node files and edge files (but it doesn't support an index mechanism). They experimented with different in-memory representations, Snapshot-Graph(SG) that stores the graph as individual snapshots, MultiGraph(MG) that stores one single graph by storing one vertex for all periods and one edge for every time period and OneGraph that stores each edge and vertex only once (also exists MGC and OGC). It has distributed locality like Immortalgraph, experimenting with different partitioning methods (the equi-depth partinioning is more efficient in most experiments) but stores materialized node/edges instead of deltas and they also experimented with both structural and temporal locality, concluding that temporal locality is more efficient (among other reasons due to the lack of sufficient discrimination in the temporal ranges of the datasets).

ImmortalGraph. [30] is a parallel in-memory storage and computation system for multicore machines and distributed settings designed for historical graphs. It focuses more on locality optimizations, both in saving the data and in the execution of the queries using locality-aware batch scheduling (LABS). They make a clear distinction and a very nice discussion between the time-centric layout and the structure-centric layout. It supports parallel temporal graph mining using iterative computations while they prefer those computations to be in memory. ImmortalGraph supports both global and local queries at a point in time or a time window. Data are stored in snapshot groups with the use either of edge files or vertex files, depending on the application. A snapshot group organizes together snapshots of a time interval by storing the first one and the changes that happened to the rest. This can be stored either with the use of time locality by grouping activities associated with a vertex (and a vertex index) or with the use of structure locality by storing together neighboring vertex (and a time index). Instead of choosing between the possible trade-off from structure and time locality, they replicate the needed data and decide which technique to use according to the type of query and how far is the starting point from the start of the snapshot group. LABS favors partition-parallelism from snapshot-parallelism, so they prefer batch operations of vertex/edges achieving better locality and less inter-core communication. They also experimented with iterative graph mining and iterative computations. In the former they reconstruct the needed snapshots in memory favoring time locality (and they compare both push, pull, and stream techniques), while in the latter they compute the first snapshot and the later $N - 1$ snapshots in batch (achieving better locality). They also implemented both low-level and high-level query interfaces, the latter used for iterative computations. An earlier implementation of ImmortalGraph is Chronos [13] with the main difference being that it only focuses on time locality. Finally, they provide a low-level as well as a high-level programming interface (APIs) that in fact define their analytics engine. They also experiment on Pagerank, diameter, SSSP, connected components, maximal independent sets, and sparse-matrix vector multiplication.

Historical Graph Store (HGS). [21] is a cloud parallel node-centric distributed system for managing and analyzing historical graphs. HGS consists of two major components, Temporal Graph Index (TGI) that manages the storage of the graph in a distributed Cassandra environment, and Temporal Graph Analysis Framework (TAF) that is a spark-based library for analyzing the graph in a cluster environment. TGI combines Partitioned Eventlists, which stores atomic changes, with Derived Partitioned Snapshots, which is a tree structure where each parent is the intersection of children deltas (used for better structure locality storing neighborhoods), both of them are partitioned, while they are also combined with Version Chain to maintain pointers to all references of nodes in chronological order. TGI divides the graph into time spans (like snapshot groups of ImmortalGraph) with micro-deltas which are stored as key-value pairs contiguously into horizontal partitions at every time span. In that way, it can execute in parallel every query to many Query Processors and aggregate the result to Query Manager or to client. It can work both on hash-based and locality-aware partitioning by projecting a time range (time-span) of the graph in a static graph. TAF supports both point in time queries and time-window, some of the supported queries are subgraph retrieval with filtering, aggregations, pattern matching, and queries about the evolution of the graph. An earlier implementation of TGI is DeltaGraph [20] which focuses on snapshot retrieval

ChronoGraph. [5] is a temporal property graph database built by extending Tinkerpop and its graph traversal language Gremlin so as to support temporal queries. It stores the temporal graph in persistent storage (MongoDB), and then loads the graph in-memory and traverses it. Their innovation is not in the storage model but in how they support traversal queries efficiently on top of it. It exploits parallelism, the temporal support of Tinkerpop to increase efficiency, and lazy evaluations to reduce memory footprints of traversals. Its main focus is on temporal graph traversals but can also return snapshots of the graph. They distinguish point-based events and period-based events because of their semantics and their architectural needs. They use aggregation to convert point-based events to period-based events so as not to have two different semantics in order to improve time efficiency in query execution. They achieve this by using a threshold as the max time interval that might exist between time instants so as to group them. A graph is composed of a static graph, a time-instant property graph, and a time-period property graph. They also use event logic, where an event might be either a vertex or an edge, on a period or a time instant. They applied temporal implementation of BFS, SSSP, and DFS, while they don't recommend DFS on their system because of Gremlins recursive logic. One more thing they discuss is that when you store the temporal graph in snapshots there will be some loss of information because a snapshot might contain data of an hour, day e.t.c according to the needs of the problem, while when you store them using time interval, you have a more accurate representation of the graph. An extension of Chronograph by using time-centric computation for traversals is given in [4].

Tink. [26] is an open-source parallel distributed temporal graph analytics library built on top of the Dataset API of Apache Flink and uses Gelly as a language. It extends the temporal property graph-model focusing on keeping intervals instead of time-points by saving nodes as tuples. It depends on Flink to use parallelism, optimizations, fault tolerance, and lazy-loading and supports iterative processing. It also uses functions from Flink like filtering, mapping, joining, and grouping. Most algorithms use Gelly's Signal/Collect (scatter-gather) model which executes computations in a vertex-centric way. It also provides temporal analytics metrics and algorithms. For the latter, they implemented shortest path earliest arrival time and shortest path fastest path while for temporal metrics they provide temporal betweenness and temporal closeness.

Gradoop (TPGM). TPGM [6,35,36] is an extension of Gradoop's EPGM model (model for static graph processing, presented in a series of papers from 2015, e.g., see [19]) to support temporal analytics on evolving property graphs (or collection of graphs) that can be used through Java API or with KNIME. Gradoop is an open-source parallel distributed dataflow framework that runs on shared-nothing clusters and uses GRALA as a declarative analytical language and Temporal-GDL as a query language. Gradoop supports Apache HBase, and Apache Accumulo to provide storage capabilities on top of HDFS, while other databases can also be used with some extra work. TPGM supports bitemporal time by adding to vertex, and edges as well as to graph the logical attributes for start and end time for both valid and transaction time (but it allows to not use some of them). While TPGM provides an abstraction, Apache Flink is used for handling the execution process in a lazy way and it provides several libraries. GRALA provides operators both for single graphs and graph collections, it supports retrieval of snapshots, transformations of attributes or properties, subgraph extraction, the difference of two snapshots, time-dependent graph grouping, temporal pattern matching, and others. For some more complex algorithms, it also supports iterative execution using Apache Flink's Gelly library.

Lastly, they have implemented a set of operations for their analytics engine and have implemented them in Flink - by using Flink Gelly. For further investigation, it should be mentioned that they provide an extensive description of their architecture while they also provide a *Lessons Learned* section that contains valuable information with respect to their design choices.

SystemG-MV. In [40] they propose an OLTP-oriented distributed temporal property graph database (dynamically evolving temporal graphs). It is built on top of IBM's SystemG, which is a distributed graph database using LMDB (B-tree based key-value store). Data are stored in tables with key/value pairs allowing to query part of the graph efficiently without retrieving whole snapshots. Different tables exist for vertices, edges, and properties, while it supports updates only on present/future timestamps like transaction-time models. Therefore, changing previous values of the graph is not allowed explicitly, but it is possible to change past events by using low-level methods. In this model, they save two timestamps for the creation/deletion of vertices/edges but while they don't allow edges to be recreated with the same id, although multiple edges can exist between a pair of vertices. For vertices, they keep the deleted vertices in a different table, while for properties they keep it simplified by keeping only one timestamp for the update as the rest can be calculated. Alongside the historic tables, they keep one table with the current state of the graph for more efficient queries.

GraphOne. [24] is an in-memory data store with a durability guarantee on external non-volatile memory NVMe SSD, while it was solely implemented in C++. Its objective is to be able to perform both real-time analytics or diverse data access while synchronous updates are applied to the database. To achieve that, GraphOne uses a hybrid model which is composed of a circular edge log and an adjacency store. The adjacency store has a multi-versioned degree array and an adjacency list with chained edges, which is used to permanently store the data taking regard to snapshots. On the other hand, edge log is used to temporary store the incoming data as edges so as to later move them in parallel to the adjacency store and improve the ingestion time. In brief, an epoch in GraphOne is consisted of 4 stages logging, archiving, durable, and compaction. At logging phases, records are inserted in the edge log at their arrival order, when the inserted edges reach the archiving threshold the multi-threaded archiving phase starts in parallel with the logging phase. At the start of the archiving phase, it shards non-archived edges to multiple local buffers so as to keep the data ordering intact, then the edges are being archived in parallel to the adjacency store, while also new degree nodes are allocated. In short, in the durable phase data are being appended to a file, while in the compaction phase deleted data are being removed. One thing that needs to be noticed is that GraphOne despite that is designed to store evolving graphs, it is not designed for getting arbitrary historic views from the adjacency store.

TEGRA. [17] is a distributed system with a compact in-memory representation (using their own storage model) both for graph and intermediate state. Its main focus is on time window analytics for historical graphs, but it can also be used for live analytics as the data are ingested in the database. An interesting feature is the ICE computational model that takes advantage of the intermediate state of computations saving it, so as to use it in the same or different queries. Computations are being made only in subgraphs affected by updates at each iteration. This has some overhead on finding the correct state and also the extra entities that should be included in the query when there is large number of updates at each iteration or while trying to use ICE on different queries. Tegra also uses TimeLapse, an API for high-level abstraction which also allows what-if questions that change the graph creating different histories, suited for data analytics purposes. The storage model behind TEGRA is DGSI, which uses persistent data structures to maintain previous versions of data when modified. It uses persistent adaptive radix trees to store edges and nodes separately with path copying. It uses simple partitioning strategies to distribute the graph to nodes. Each node has two pART for nodes and edges respectively. Log files are being used to store updates between snapshots, which are stored in turn in the two pARTs. The branch and commit primitives are really interesting as well as the GAS (Gather - Apply - Scatter) model [11]. It allows also changing any version thus leading to a branched history (like a tree - full persistence). Lastly, TEGRA also uses an LRU policy to periodically remove versions that have not been accessed for a long time.

STVG. [28] is a prototype framework that focuses on fast-evolving graphs. It is built on top of Neo4j and supports both point and time-window queries while its main use is to analyze evolutionary transit networks. It is based on the whole-graph model for representing the graph, which is composed of subgraphs that facilitate the conceptual modeling of the connectivity between entities and the time-graph of Neo4j that is responsible for keeping track of time evolution. Subgraphs are connected to the time-graph to keep track of the evolution of the whole-graph, while nodes belonging to different subgraphs are linked with complementary connectivity edges. Since this framework is used for evolutionary transit networks it is demanded that the graph needs to be connected while edges can't recur over time. Projected graphs are used to materialize and retrieve the graph both at a time-window or a sliding window. They have implemented also graph metrics used to analyze a transit network, graph density, network diameter, and average path length having in mind their specific application. In general, this framework has some good ideas but it is tailored for transit networks.

Graphite. [9] is a distributed system for managing historical graphs (fully evolved and using valid time) by using an interval-centric computing model (ICM) built over Apache Giraph. They assume data are given in ascending time order and any vertex can exist only once for a contiguous time-interval. It also has the ability to execute both time-independent and time-dependant historical queries (temporal queries on a time-window), while they tried to create a unifying abstraction that scales to both and ease algorithm design and detach user logic using ICM and time-warp operator. ICM uses Bulk Synchronous Parallel (BSP) execution for every active vertex of a query until it converges. They use two stages of logic, compute and scatter, where compute does the computations needed for a vertex, and scatter transfers it with messages to neighbor vertexes as needed. Time-warp operator happens at the alternating compute scatter steps to help sharing of calls and messages across intervals. A key aspect of it, is that it groups input guaranteeing correctness of grouping and no duplication, while it returns as minimal as possible triples. They also designed and constructed a plethora of time independent (TI) and time dependent (TD) algorithms for their system. with a very detailed evaluation

Granite. [34] is a distributed engine for storing and analyzing temporal property graphs (supports temporal path queries) made on top of and as a sequel to Graphite focusing on path queries. It is made an assumption for infrequent updates and frequent queries. They extend the previous model by adding a temporal aggregation operator, indexing, query planning and optimization, while they prefer to relax ICM so as to work beyond time respecting algorithms. Granite handles both static temporal graphs and dynamic temporal graphs while it uses interval-centric features only in the latter. An interesting point is that to optimize path queries they split them and execute them concurrently, while they also keep statistics about the active nodes at each time point so as to optimize the query planning. While Graphite makes hash partitioning at query execution, Granite first partitions every entity according to its type and later it performs a topological partition to its independent group of entities of the same type and splits them into workers using the round-robin technique. They also use a result tree so as not to send duplicate paths across the system (some parts of the path might be the same). Lastly, they propose a query language for path queries.

NVGRAPH. A rather interesting system from a hardware perspective. NVGRAPH [27] is an in-memory data structure focused on exploiting the different advantages of NVMM and DRAM, combining them into a C++ library implementation. The major issue they try to tackle in NVMM is providing crash consistency while they argue that simply using NVMM without considering its issues is a sub-optimal solution. They focus on creating an architecture that uses both DRAM and NVMM to hide the issues of NVMM while they are exploiting its advantages. NVGraph stores the graph as a series of continuous snapshots by storing the first snapshot and deltas for the next snapshots. They also implemented 4 algorithms for evaluation Pagerank, BFS, influence maximization, and rumor source detection.

3   Architecture of MAGMA

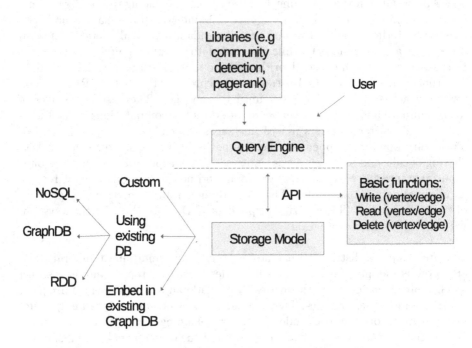

Fig. 1. A view of MAGMA with the possible storage directions.

In this section, we describe the general characteristics of the proposed historical graph management and processing system (MAGMA), the possible directions we could take implementing it as well as the possible obstacles we need to
overcome.

An immediate observation from the previous systems is that each one of
them focuses on different aspects of historical graph management, resulting in
a different appropriate solution for each application. This is because the management and processing of historical graphs span multiple design dimensions
forbidding the existence of one system to rule them all. Our approach is towards
creating a purely vertex-centric and storage optimal (asymptotically) distributed
system called MAGMA with the ability to update/query efficiently the history
and apply graph algorithms on arbitrary time periods rather than on specified snapshots. Following HiNode, MAGMA will be more efficient in local than
global queries due to its vertex-centric structure. However, we also wish to efficiently execute global queries (e.g., pagerank) by exploiting our vertex-centric
architecture and implementing modern techniques (e.g., thinking like a vertex)
for efficient and effective parallel computation. Another important aspect that
needs to be addressed in a later stage of the development of MAGMA, is the

system's API. In particular, we need to design the system in a way that guarantees its simplicity with respect to use, its efficiency, its scalability, its flexibility with respect to its functionality, and its compatibility with existing libraries (for static or temporal graphs).

The key part of the system is the efficient and effective vertex-centric storage of the graph. A diachronic node contains the whole history of a particular node in the sense that it stores all changes and their time intervals related to this node, such as a change in an incoming edge or a change in a property of the node. To this end, we employ three fundamental operations in order to update and query the diachronic nodes: write, read and delete. All three operations are applied on diachronic nodes that contain all relevant information (edges, properties, etc.). More complex updates and query operations can be built on these fundamental operations that will serve mainly the online management and processing of the historical graph.

Regarding the storage model, we have narrowed our options into either creating a custom database for storing the historical graph into servers or by extending an existing database and applying our model to them. In any case, we will always stick to the pure vertex-centric approach proposed in HiNode and adapt it appropriately to fit the design choice of the storage model. In the case of creating a custom database, we have complete freedom with respect to designing the storage model to fit HiNode, but on the other hand, it will require considerably more effort for the implementation as well as to ensure compatibility with existing libraries. On the other hand one could use an existing database, either a NoSQL database like Cassandra and MongoDB or a Graph database (e.g., GraphX and SystemG). In this case, it is easier to build the system and take advantage of the optimizations and functionality that already exist within this database (e.g., fault-tolerance and partitioning), but there is less freedom in applying the storage model of HiNode. Another option, in this case, is to extend an existing graph database (e.g., GraphX) to support natively the management and processing of historical graphs based on a pure vertex-centric approach. This is a harder task, but it has the merit of sharing and using existing libraries within this particular graph database. In addition, the visibility of such a solution will be much higher across the community.

Since MAGMA is a distributed system, the partitioning strategy is of paramount importance for the efficiency of the system. Most systems use either a simple hash-based partition or a chronological or topological partitioning. In our case, the topological partitioning is more natural but we also need to take into account the temporal evolution of the graph. In topological partitioning, we want to place in the same machine, nodes that are connected or that are relatively close to each other. One problem we might encounter with topological partitioning is that in different timestamps, the distance between nodes changes, and as a result, different partitions may be more appropriate in different time instances. This is problematic in our case since a diachronic node contains all the history of the node and thus naturally all history is stored in a single machine. Two possible solutions for this issue are either by using different metrics for partitioning combining the whole history of the graph or by dividing parts of a node to different machines. Another possible solution, which could also be combined with the previous one, is the duplication of some nodes across machines. However, in this case, care should be taken with respect to space usage.

Another critical part of the system is the query engine and the libraries that will be available. Regarding the libraries, we intend to implement algorithms on temporal graphs like temporal shortest path (journeys) or community detection and evolution while also supporting algorithms for static snapshots. This can be achieved either by using the abstraction provided from the API or by exploiting the system's architecture and creating them from scratch. For the former task, we first want to create a query engine able to handle more demanding tasks that supports parallelism and provides the user with an easy-to-use API. To do so, our processing unit needs to apply one of the following approaches: "thinking like an edge" (TLAE), "thinking like a vertex" (TLEV), "thinking like a neighborhood" (TLAN), "thinking like a subgraph" (TLAS) or "thinking like an interval" (TLAI). We need to further investigate these approaches and decide which one would be more efficient in our system, although we can deduce straightforwardly that some of these will probably not fit our vertex-centric architecture. On the other hand, TLEV techniques seem as the most promising at the moment, in order to take advantage of Hinode's vertex-centric structure, while TLAN or TLAS approaches could also fit our model depending on the partition strategy used. At a later stage, these approaches will be used for iterative computations.

4 Conclusions

In this paper, we provide a small review of contemporary historical graph management systems and propose an architecture for such a system based on our previous research work. We intend to extend the very preliminary results contained in this paper as follows: 1) A survey on systems for historical graph management. This survey will cover all historical graph management systems and will provide researchers as well as developers information as to the pros and cons of these systems in order to help them choose correctly. 2) The development of a system (called MAGMA) for managing and processing historical graphs. The high-level architecture of this system and basic options for its implementation are described in this paper.

References

1. Andriamampianina, L., Ravat, F., Song, J., Vallès-Parlangeau, N.: A generic modelling to capture the temporal evolution in graphs. In: 16e journées EDA : Business Intelligence & Big Data (EDA 2020), vol. RNTI-B-16, pp. 19–32. Lyon, France (2020). https://hal.science/hal-03109670
2. Besta, M., Fischer, M., Kalavri, V., Kapralov, M., Hoefler, T.: Practice of streaming processing of dynamic graphs: concepts, models, and systems (2021)

3. Bok, K., Kim, G., Lim, J., Yoo, J.: Historical graph management in dynamic environments. Electronics **9**(6), 895 (2020). https://doi.org/10.3390/electronics9060895

4. Byun, J.: Enabling time-centric computation for efficient temporal graph traversals from multiple sources. IEEE Transactions on Knowledge and Data Engineering, p. 1 (2020). https://doi.org/10.1109/TKDE.2020.3005672

5. Byun, J., Woo, S., Kim, D.: Chronograph: enabling temporal graph traversals for efficient information diffusion analysis over time. IEEE Trans. Knowl. Data Eng. **32**(3), 424–437 (2020). https://doi.org/10.1109/TKDE.2019.2891565

6. Christ, L., Gomez, K., Rahm, E., Peukert, E.: Distributed graph pattern matching on evolving graphs (2020)

7. Dhulipala, L., Blelloch, G.E., Shun, J.: Low-latency graph streaming using compressed purely-functional trees. In: Proceedings of the 40th ACM SIGPLAN Conference on Programming Language Design and Implementation, pp. 918–934. PLDI 2019, Association for Computing Machinery, New York, NY, USA (2019)

8. Ding, M., Yang, M., Chen, S.: Storing and querying large-scale spatio-temporal graphs with high-throughput edge insertions. arXiv preprint arXiv:1904.09610 (2019)

9. Gandhi, S., Simmhan, Y.: An interval-centric model for distributed computing over temporal graphs. In: 2020 IEEE 36th International Conference on Data Engineering (ICDE), pp. 1129–1140 (2020). https://doi.org/10.1109/ICDE48307.2020.00102

10. Gedik, B., Bordawekar, R.: Disk-based management of interaction graphs. IEEE Trans. Knowl. Data Eng. **26**(11), 2689–2702 (2014). https://doi.org/10.1109/TKDE.2013.2297930

11. Gonzalez, J.E., Low, Y., Gu, H., Bickson, D., Guestrin, C.: PowerGraph: distributed graph-parallel computation on natural graphs, pp. 17–30. OSDI2012, USENIX Association (2012)

12. Han, W., Li, K., Chen, S., Chen, W.: Auxo: a temporal graph management system. Big Data Min. Anal. **2**(1), 58–71 (2019). https://doi.org/10.26599/BDMA.2018.9020030

13. Han, W., et al.: Chronos: a graph engine for temporal graph analysis. In: Proceedings of the Ninth European Conference on Computer Systems. EuroSys 2014, Association for Computing Machinery, New York, NY, USA (2014). https://doi.org/10.1145/2592798.2592799

14. Hartmann, T., Fouquet, F., Jimenez, M., Rouvoy, R., Le Traon, Y.: Analyzing complex data in motion at scale with temporal graphs (2017). https://doi.org/10.18293/SEKE2017-048

15. Huang, H., Song, J., Lin, X., Ma, S., Huai, J.: TGraph: a temporal graph data management system. In: Proceedings of the 25th ACM International on Conference on Information and Knowledge Management, pp. 2469–2472. CIKM 2016, Association for Computing Machinery, New York, NY, USA (2016). https://doi.org/10.1145/2983323.2983335

16. Iyer, A.P., Li, L.E., Das, T., Stoica, I.: Time-evolving graph processing at scale. In: Proceedings of the Fourth International Workshop on Graph Data Management Experiences and Systems, pp. 1–6 (2016)

17. Iyer, A.P., Pu, Q., Patel, K., Gonzalez, J.E., Stoica, I.: TEGRA: efficient ad-hoc analytics on evolving graphs. In: 18th USENIX Symposium on Networked Systems Design and Implementation (NSDI 21), pp. 337–355. USENIX Association (2021). https://www.usenix.org/conference/nsdi21/presentation/iyer

18. Ju, X., Williams, D., Jamjoom, H., Shin, K.G.: Version traveler: fast and memory-efficient version switching in graph processing systems. In: 2016 USENIX Annual Technical Conference (USENIX-ATC 16), pp. 523–536 (2016)
19. Junghanns, M., Petermann, A., Teichmann, N., Gómez, K., Rahm, E.: Analyzing extended property graphs with apache flink. In: Proceedings of the 1st ACM SIGMOD Workshop on Network Data Analytics. NDA 2016, Association for Computing Machinery, New York, NY, USA (2016). https://doi.org/10.1145/2980523.2980527
20. Khurana, U., Deshpande, A.: Efficient snapshot retrieval over historical graph data. In: 2013 IEEE 29th International Conference on Data Engineering (ICDE), pp. 997–1008 (2013). https://doi.org/10.1109/ICDE.2013.6544892
21. Khurana, U., Deshpande, A.: Storing and analyzing historical graph data at scale. In: Pitoura, E., et al. (eds.) Proceedings of the 19th International Conference on Extending Database Technology, EDBT 2016, Bordeaux, France, 15–16 March 2016, pp. 65–76. OpenProceedings.org (2016). https://doi.org/10.5441/002/edbt.2016.09
22. Kosmatopoulos, A., Gounaris, A., Tsichlas, K.: Hinode: implementing a vertex-centric modelling approach to maintaining historical graph data. Computing **101**(12), 1885–1908 (2019)
23. Kosmatopoulos, A., Tsichlas, K., Gounaris, A., Sioutas, S., Pitoura, E.: Hinode: an asymptotically space-optimal storage model for historical queries on graphs. Distrib. Parall. Databases **35**(3–4), 249–285 (2017)
24. Kumar, P., Huang, H.H.: GraphOne: a data store for real-time analytics on evolving graphs. ACM Trans. Storage **15**(4) (2020). https://doi.org/10.1145/3364180
25. Labouseur, A.G., et al.: The g* graph database: efficiently managing large distributed dynamic graphs. Distrib. Parall. Databases **33**(4), 479–514 (2015)
26. Lightenberg, W., Pei, Y., Fletcher, G., Pechenizkiy, M.: Tink: A temporal graph analytics library for apache Flink. In: Companion Proceedings of the The Web Conference 2018, pp. 71–72 (2018)
27. Lim, S., Coy, T., Lu, Z., Ren, B., Zhang, X.: NVGraph: enforcing crash consistency of evolving network analytics in NVMM systems. IEEE Trans. Parall. Distrib. System. **31**(6), 1255–1269 (2020). https://doi.org/10.1109/TPDS.2020.2965452
28. Maduako, I., Wachowicz, M., Hanson, T.: STVG: an evolutionary graph framework for analyzing fast-evolving networks. J. Big Data **6**(1), 1–24 (2019)
29. Massri, M., Raipin Parvedy, P., Meye, P.: GDBAlive: a temporal graph database built on top of a columnar data store. J. Adv. Inf. Technol. **12**, 169–178 (2020). https://doi.org/10.12720/jait.12.3.169-178
30. Miao, Y., et al.: ImmortalGraph: a system for storage and analysis of temporal graphs. ACM Trans. Storage **11**(3), 2700302 (2015). https://doi.org/10.1145/2700302
31. Moffitt, V., Stoyanovich, J.: Portal: a query language for evolving graphs (2016)
32. Moffitt, V.Z.: Framework for querying and analysis of evolving graphs, Ph. D. thesis (2017). https://doi.org/10.13140/RG.2.2.16079.64166. https://www.proquest.com/docview/1946186055?pq-origsite=gscholar&fromopenview=true
33. Moffitt, V.Z., Stoyanovich, J.: Towards sequenced semantics for evolving graphs. In: EDBT, pp. 446–449 (2017)
34. Ramesh, S., Baranawal, A., Simmhan, Y.: Granite: a distributed engine for scalable path queries over temporal property graphs. J. Parallel Distrib. Comput. **151**, 94–111 (2021)
35. Rost, C., et al.: Distributed temporal graph analytics with GRADOOP. VLDB J. **31**, 375–401 (2021). https://doi.org/10.1007/s00778-021-00667-4

36. Rost, C., Thor, A., Rahm, E.: Analyzing temporal graphs with GRADOOP. Datenbank-Spektrum **19**(3), 199–208 (2019)
37. Sahu, S., Salihoglu, S.: Graphsurge: Graph analytics on view collections using differential computation. In: Proceedings of the 2021 International Conference on Management of Data, pp. 1518–1530 (2021)
38. Spitalas, A., Gounaris, A., Tsichlas, K., Kosmatopoulos, A.: Investigation of database models for evolving graphs. In: Combi, C., Eder, J., Reynolds, M. (eds.) 28th International Symposium on Temporal Representation and Reasoning, TIME 2021, 27–29 September 2021, Klagenfurt, Austria. LIPIcs, vol. 206, pp. 1–13. Schloss Dagstuhl - Leibniz-Zentrum für Informatik (2021). https://doi.org/10.4230/LIPIcs.TIME.2021.6
39. Steer, B., Cuadrado, F., Clegg, R.: Raphtory: streaming analysis of distributed temporal graphs. Future Gener. Comput. Syst. **102**, 453–464 (2020)
40. Vijitbenjaronk, W.D., Lee, J., Suzumura, T., Tanase, G.: Scalable time-versioning support for property graph databases. In: 2017 IEEE International Conference on Big Data (Big Data), pp. 1580–1589 (2017). https://doi.org/10.1109/BigData.2017.8258092
41. Zaki, A., Attia, M., Hegazy, D., Amin, S.: Comprehensive survey on dynamic graph models. Int. J. Adv. Comput. Sci. Appl. **7**(2), 573–582 (2016)

New Results in Priority-Based Bin Packing

K. Subramani[1]([⊠]), P. Wojciechowski[1], and Alvaro Velasquez[2]

[1] LDCSEE, West Virginia University, Morgantown, WV, USA
k.subramani@mail.wvu.edu, pwojciec@mix.wvu.edu
[2] Department of Computer Science, University of Colorado at Boulder, Boulder, USA
alvaro.velasquez@colorado.edu

Abstract. In this paper, we discuss new algorithmic results for bin minimization in the subset-constrained variant of Priority-based bin packing (PBBP-SC). This problem was introduced in [21], as an abstract model for capturing certain issues in database migration and palleting. This paper focuses on new fine-grained complexity results for the bin minimization problem (BMP) under two distinct parameterizations. We also provide a detailed empirical analysis of integer programming formulations for the problems discussed in this paper.

1 Introduction

This paper is concerned with the design and analysis (both theoretical and empirical) of the bin minimization problem (BMP) in the Priority-based bin packing with subset constraints (PBBP-SC) problem. The PBBP-SC problem was introduced in [21] and finds applications in Security Aware Database Migration (SADM) [1,18,19], palleting [2,14] and a host of other domains, where there are constraints restricting the placement of items into bins.

Typically, when companies merge, their data must be unified in some fashion. Data migration is a process that achieves precisely this end [11–13]. Data migration involves transferring data between storage types and computer systems [7,9]. The migration process is labor-intensive and hence companies prefer to automate the process [5] and free up human resources. Database migration is a variant of the data migration problem in which the data have to be migrated in form-preserving fashion. For instance, if the data is stored in relational databases, then the databases themselves have to be migrated. A variant of the database migration problem is the Security Aware Database Migration problem (henceforth SADM). This problem was introduced in [18]. In this problem, we are given a collection of databases (D_i) of various sizes that need to be assigned to migration shifts (S_i). The shifts have varying sizes themselves. Furthermore, each database is constrained by the shifts to which it can be assigned. This feature models the fact that the expertise for addressing the issues associated with a database can be found only in certain shifts. For instance, it could be the case

L. Foschini and S. Kontogiannis (Eds.): ALGOCLOUD 2022, LNCS 13799, pp. 58–72, 2023.
https://doi.org/10.1007/978-3-031-33437-5_4

that database D_1 can be migrated only in shifts S_4 and S_7. We need to assign the databases to the shifts so that these shift assignment constraints for each item are met. At the same time, we wish to minimize the number of shifts used in the assignment, since shifts correspond to man-hours used and are therefore expensive.

The palleting problem (also known as the Pallet Loading Problem (PLP) is a fundamental problem in Air-Force logistics [14]. The objective in pallet loading is to maximize the number of boxes that can be placed on a rectangular pallet [17]. This problem can be thought of as a cross between the traditional bin-packing problem and the traditional knapsack problem [3, 16]. The palleting problem also involves object to pallet constraints, i.e., each object has a set of pallets onto which it can be loaded.

A formal framework for the specification of database problems was specified in [19]. That paper focused exclusively on test-cost minimization. In [18], the security-aware database migration problem was introduced. The Priority-based bin packing model was detailed in [21]. In this paper, we extend the work in [21] by considering the fine-grained complexity of bin minimization problems in the PBBP-SC framework.

As is the case with traditional bin-packing (TBP), the problem of minimizing the number of used bins in Priority-based bin packing is also **NP-hard** [10, 21]. In the case of **NP-hard** problems, a profitable avenue of investigation is fine-grained complexity [4, 6, 8]. In case of traditional bin-packing, it is not profitable to investigate the design of efficient algorithms using the number of bins as a parameter [15]. This is because it is **NP-hard** to decide whether 2 bins are adequate to pack the given items in an instance of TBP. In this paper, we use alternate parameterizations and show that it is unlikely that the BMP variant of PBBP-SC will have fixed parameter algorithms.

The rest of this paper is organized as follows: A formal description of the problems under consideration in this paper is given in Sect. 2. Two distinct parameterizations of the bin minimization problem and their associated complexities are discussed in Sect. 3. We discuss integer programming formulations for BMP and a number of cuts in Sect. 4. A detailed empirical profile of integer programming approaches for the BMP problem is provided in Sect. 5. We conclude in Sect. 6, by summarizing our contributions and outlining avenues for future research.

2   Statement of Problems

As defined in [21], an instance of Priority-based Bin Packing with Subset Constraints (PBBP-SC) consists of the following:

1. A set of bins $\mathbf{B}$ where each bin $b_j \in \mathbf{B}$ has capacity c_j.
2. A set of unit-size items $\mathbf{O}$ where each item $o_i \in \mathbf{O}$ has priority p_i.
3. For each item $o_i \in \mathbf{O}$, a set $B_i \subseteq \mathbf{B}$ such that item o_i can be packed into any bin in the set B_i, but not into any bin in the set $\mathbf{B} \setminus B_i$.

There are several problems associated with PBBP-SC. These are the feasibility problem (FP), the priority maximization problem (PMP), and the bin-minimization problem (BMP). These problems are defined as follows:

Definition 1 (FP). *The* **Feasibility Problem (FP)***: Given a PBBP-SC instance* **P***, can we pack the items in set* **O** *into the bins in set B such that, every item $o_i \in$* **O** *is packed into a bin in set B_i, and every bin b_j contains no more than c_j items?*

Definition 2 (PMP). *The* **Priority Maximization Problem (PMP)***: Given a PBBP-SC instance* **P***, what is the maximum total priority of items in set O that can be packed into the bins in set* **B***, such that every item $o_i \in$* **O** *can only be packed into bins in set B_i, and every bin b_j contains no more than c_j items?*

Definition 3 (BMP). *The* **Bin Minimization Problem (BMP)***: Given a PBBP-SC instance* **P***, what is the smallest cardinality subset $B^* \subseteq$* **B** *such that every item $o_i \in$* **O** *is packed into a bin in set $B_i \cap B^*$, and every bin b_j contains no more than c_j items?*

In this paper, we focus exclusively on the **BMP** problem. The three principal contributions of this paper are as follows:

1. BMP is **W[2]-complete** when parameterized by the minimum number of bins used in any packing.
2. BMP is **paraNP-complete** when parameterized by the maximum number of items that can be packed into a bin ($\max_{b_j \in \mathbf{B}} |\{o_i | b_j \in B_i\}|$).
3. An empirical analysis of several cuts for an integer programming formulation of BMP.

3   BMP Parameterizations

In this section, we examine the parameterized complexity of BMP under two different parameters. These are:

P1: The minimum number of bins used in any packing.
P2: The maximum number of items that can be packed into a bin
     ($\max_{b_j \in \mathbf{B}} |\{o_i | b_j \in B_i\}|$).

3.1   BMP Parameterized by P1

We now examine BMP when parameterized by the minimum number of bins used. We show that BMP is **W[2]-complete** under this parameter. This is done by reductions to and from the Set Cover (SC) problem. It is known that SC is **W[2]-complete**, when parameterized by the number of sets in the minimal cover (see Theorem 13.28 of [6]).

Definition 4. *Set Cover: Given a set S of size n, m subsets S_1 through S_m of S, and an integer k, is there a set $C \subseteq \{1, \ldots, m\}$ such that $|C| \leq k$ and $\bigcup_{j \in C} S_j = S$?*

Let SC be an instance of set cover. From SC, we construct a PBBP-SC instance **P** as follows:

1. For each subset S_j, create the bin b_j. Let $c_j = |S_j|$.
2. For each element $x_i \in S$, create the item o_i. Let $B_i = \{b_j | x_i \in S_j\}$.

Lemma 1. *Let SC be an instance of set cover and let P be the PBBP-SC instance constructed from SC. SC has a cover of size at most k, if and only if P has a packing using at most k bins.*

Proof. First, assume that SC has a cover C such that $|C| \leq k$. We create a packing of **P** as follows: For each item o_i, let $S_j \in C$ be a set such that $x_i \in S_j$. Since C is a cover, this set is guaranteed to exist. Pack item o_i into bin b_j.

We now show that this is a valid packing for P. Note that the item o_i is packed into bin b_j, only if $x_i \in S_j$. By construction, $b_j \in B_i$. Thus, each item is packed into a valid bin. The capacity c_j of bin b_j is equal to the size of set S_j. Thus, there are at most c_j items packed into bin b_j. Consequently, the packing does not fill any bin beyond its capacity. This means that we have constructed a valid packing for P. Note that a bin b_j is used by the packing, only if the set $S_j \in C$. Thus, this packing uses at most $|C| \leq k$ bins.

Now assume that **P** has a packing using at most k bins. We create a cover C of SC as follows: For every set S_j, add j to C, if and only if the bin b_j is used by the packing of P. Consider the element $x_i \in S$. The item o_i was packed into a bin b_j such that $x_i \in S_j$. By construction, $j \in C$. Consequently, the element x_i is covered by C. Since the element $x_i \in S$ was chosen arbitrarily, C is a cover of SC. Note that the number of sets in C is the number of bins used by the packing. Since the packing uses at most k bins $|C| \leq k$ as desired. □

The SC problem is **W[2]-complete** when parameterized by the number of sets in the cover. Thus, we have the following result.

Theorem 1. *BMP is **W[2]-hard** when parameterized by the minimum number of bins used.*

Proof. The SC problem is **W[2]-complete** when parameterized by the number of sets in the cover. Thus, by Lemma 1, BMP is **W[2]-hard** when parameterized by the minimum number of bins used. □

To show that BMP is in **W[2]**, we reduce BMP to the SC problem. From a PBBP-SC instance **P**, we construct a set cover instance SC as follows:

1. For each item o_i, add the item x_i to S.
2. For each bin b_j, create the set $S_j = \{x_i | b_j \in B_i\}$.

Lemma 2. *Let* **P** *be a PBBP-SC instance and let SC be the set cover instance constructed from* **P**. *SC has a cover of size at most k, if and only if P has a packing using at most k bins.*

Proof. First, assume that **P** has a packing using at most k bins. We create a cover C of SC as follows: For every set S_j, add j to C, if and only if the bin b_j is used by the packing of P. Consider the element $x_i \in S$. The item o_i was packed into a bin b_j such that $x_i \in S_j$. By construction, $j \in C$. Consequently, the element x_i is covered by C. Since the element $x_i \in S$ was chosen arbitrarily, C is a cover of SC. Note that the number of sets in C is the number of bins used by the packing. Since the packing uses at most k bins $|C| \leq k$ as desired.

Now assume that SC has a cover C such that $|C| \leq k$. We create a packing of **P** as follows: For each item o_i, let $S_j \in C$ be a set such that $x_i \in S_j$. Since C is a cover, this set is guaranteed to exist. Pack item o_i into bin b_j.

We now show that this is a valid packing for P. Note that the item o_i is packed into bin b_j, only if $x_i \in S_j$. By construction, $b_j \in B_i$. Thus, each item is packed into a valid bin. Note that a bin b_j is used by the packing, only if the set $S_j \in C$. Thus, this packing uses at most $|C| \leq k$ bins. $\quad\square$

From Lemma 1 and Lemma 2, BMP is **W[2]-complete** when parameterized by the minimum number of bins used. Thus, BMP is not fixed-parameter tractable (**FPT**) unless **FPT** = **W[2]**. Note that both reductions used in this section are parameterized reductions [6].

3.2   BMP Parameterized by P2

We now examine BMP when parameterized by the maximum number of items that can be packed into a bin ($\max_{b_j \in \mathbf{B}} |\{o_i | b_j \in B_i\}|$). We show that BMP is **paraNP-complete** under this parameter. In fact, we show that BMP is **NP-complete** when $\max_{b_j \in \mathbf{B}} |\{o_i | b_j \in B_i\}| = 4$. This is done by a reduction from SAT.

Let Φ be a CNF formula, from Φ, we construct a PBBP-SC instance **P** as follows:

1. For each variable $x_i \in \Phi$, create the bins $b_{2 \cdot i - 1}$ and $b_{2 \cdot i}$. Let d_i be the number of clauses that use the variable x_i. Set $c_{2 \cdot i - 1} = c_{2 \cdot i} = d_i + 1$.
2. For each variable $x_i \in \Phi$, create the item o_i. Let $B_i = \{b_{2 \cdot i - 1}, b_{2 \cdot i}\}$.
3. For each clause ϕ_j, create the item o_{n+j}. If ϕ_j uses the literal x_i, add the bin $b_{2 \cdot i - 1}$ to B_{n+j}. If ϕ_j uses the literal $\neg x_i$, add the bin $b_{2 \cdot i}$ to B_{n+j}.

Lemma 3. *Let* Φ *be a CNF formula and let* **P** *be the PBBP-SC instance constructed from* Φ. Φ *is satisfiable, if and only if* **P** *has a packing using at most n bins.*

Proof. By construction, the sets B_1 through B_n are mutually disjoint. Thus, the items o_1 through o_n must be packed into separate bins. This means that no packing of the items in O uses fewer than n bins. Additionally, for each $i = 1 \ldots n$, either bin $b_{2 \cdot i - 1}$ or bin $b_{2 \cdot i}$ must be used.

First, assume that $\mathbf{P}$ has a packing P that uses n bins. Observe that, if for any $i = 1 \ldots n$ both bin $b_{2 \cdot i - 1}$ and bin $b_{2 \cdot i}$ are used, then P must use at least $(n + 1)$ bins. Thus, P cannot use both of these bins.

From P, we construct an assignment $\mathbf{x}$ to Φ as follows: For each $i = 1 \ldots n$

1. If P uses bin $b_{2 \cdot i - 1}$, set the variable x_i to **true**.
2. If P uses bin $b_{2 \cdot i}$, set the variable x_i to **false**.

Now consider a clause $\phi_j \in \Phi$. The item o_{n+j} is either packed into bin $b_{2 \cdot i - 1}$ or bin $b_{2 \cdot i}$ for some $i = 1 \ldots n$. If item o_{n+j} is packed into bin $b_{2 \cdot i - 1}$, then by construction, clause ϕ_j contains the literal x_i. Additionally, bin $b_{2 \cdot i - 1}$ is used by packing P. Thus, the assignment $\mathbf{x}$ sets the variable x_i to **true**. Consequently, ϕ_j contains a **true** literal and is satisfied by $\mathbf{x}$.

If item o_{n+j} is packed into bin $b_{2 \cdot i}$, then by construction, clause ϕ_j contains the literal $\neg x_i$. Additionally, bin $b_{2 \cdot i}$ is used by packing P. Thus, the assignment $\mathbf{x}$ sets the variable x_i to **false**. Consequently, ϕ_j contains a **true** literal and is satisfied by $\mathbf{x}$.

Since $\mathbf{x}$ satisfies every clause of Φ, Φ is satisfiable.

Now assume that Φ is satisfiable. Thus, there exists an assignment $\mathbf{x}$ that satisfies every clause in Φ. From $\mathbf{x}$, we construct a packing P of $\mathbf{P}$ as follows:

1. For each variable x_i, if x_i is **true**, then pack item o_i into bin $b_{2 \cdot i - 1}$. Otherwise, pack item o_i into bin $b_{2 \cdot i}$.
2. For each clause $\phi_j \in \Phi$, let l_j be a literal in ϕ_j set to **true** by $\mathbf{x}$. If l_j is the literal x_i for some variable x_i, then pack item o_{n+j} into bin $b_{2 \cdot i - 1}$. If l_j is the literal $\neg x_i$ for some variable x_i, then pack item o_{n+j} into bin $b_{2 \cdot i}$.

The constructed packing P has the following properties:

1. If $\mathbf{x}$ set the variable x_i to **true**, then the literal $\neg x_i$ is **false**. Thus, no item will be packed into bin $b_{2 \cdot i}$. If $\mathbf{x}$ set the variable x_i to **false**, then the literal x_i is **false**. Thus, no item will be packed into bin $b_{2 \cdot i - 1}$. This means that for each variable x_i, P does not use both bin $b_{2 \cdot i - 1}$ and bin $b_{2 \cdot i}$. Consequently, P uses at most n bins.
2. By construction, every item o_j in P is packed into a bin in B_j.
3. The literal x_i appears in at most d_i clauses. Thus at most $d_i + 1 = c_{2 \cdot i - 1}$ items are packed into bin $b_{2 \cdot i - 1}$. Similarly, the literal $\neg x_i$ appears in at most d_i clauses. Thus, at most $d_i + 1 = c_{2 \cdot i}$ items are packed into bin $b_{2 \cdot i}$. Consequently, no bin is packed beyond its capacity.

Thus, P is a valid packing of PBBP-SC instance $\mathbf{P}$. Consequently, $\mathbf{P}$ has a packing that uses n bins. $\qquad\square$

Note that SAT remains **NP-complete** when each variable appears in at most 3 clauses [20]. This gives us the following result.

Theorem 2. *BMP is* **paraNP-complete** *when parameterized by the maximum number of items that can be packed into a bin.*

Proof. SAT is **NP-complete** when each variable appears in at most 3 clauses [20]. Note that the construction utilized by Lemma 3 creates an instance of PBBP-SC in which each bin can hold at most 4 items. Thus, BMP is still **NP-hard** when each bin can hold at most 4 items. Consequently, BMP is **paraNP-complete** when parameterized by the maximum number of items that can be packed into a bin.   □

From this result, we know that BMP is **NP-hard** when $\max_{b_j \in \mathbf{B}} |\{o_i|b_j \in B_\ell\}| = 4$. In other words, BMP is unlikely to admit a $O(n^{f(k)})$ time algorithm where f is a computable function and $k = \max_{b_j \in \mathbf{B}} |\{o_i|b_j \in B_i\}|$.

4   Integer Programming Formulations

Given a PBBP-SC instance **P**, BMP is equivalent to the integer program $\mathbf{I_{BMP}}$ constructed as follows:

1. For each item o_i and bin b_j, if item o_i can be assigned to bin b_j ($b_j \in B_i$), then create the variable $x_{i,j} \in \{0,1\}$.
2. For each bin b_j, create the variable $y_j \in \{0,1\}$ and create the constraint $\sum_{i|b_j \in B_i} x_{i,j} \leq c_j \cdot y_j$. This constraint represents the fact that at most c_j items can be packed into bin b_j. Additionally, the variable $y_j = 1$, if any item was packed into bin b_j.
3. For each item o_i, create the constraint $\sum_{b_j \in B_i} x_{i,j} = 1$. This constraint represents the fact that item o_i has to be packed and can be packed into at most one bin.
4. Add the objective function $\min \sum_{j=1}^{m} y_j$. This objective function ensures that the number of bins used is minimized.

Theorem 3. *Let* **P** *be a PBBP-SC instance and let* $\mathbf{I_{BMP}}$ *be the integer program associated with BMP for* **P**. **P** *has a packing that uses* b^* *bins, if and only if* $\mathbf{I_{BMP}}$ *has a feasible assignment with objective value* b^*.

Proof. First, assume that **P** has a packing P that uses at most b^* bins. Let $P(o_i)$ represent the bin used to pack item o_i. From packing P, we construct an assignment $(\mathbf{x}, \mathbf{y})$ to $\mathbf{I_{BMP}}$ as follows:

1. For each item o_i, let $b_j = P(o_i)$. Set $x_{i,j} = 1$ and $x_{i,j'} = 0$ for $j' \neq j$.
2. For each bin b_j, if there is an item o_i such that $P(o_i) = b_j$, then set $y_j = 1$. Otherwise, set $y_j = 0$.

Let o_i be an item in **P**. By construction, exactly one of the $x_{i,j}$ variables is 1. Thus $\sum_{b_j \in B_i} x_{i,j} = 1$. Thus, each constraint of the form $\sum_{b_j \in B_i} x_{i,j} = 1$ in $\mathbf{I_{BMP}}$ is satisfied.

Let b_j be a bin in **P**. By construction, if any item was packed into bin b_j, $y_j = 1$. For any item o_i, if o_i was packed into b_j, $x_{i,j} = 1$. Since P packs at most c_j items into bin b_j, $\sum_{i|b_j \in B_i} x_{i,j} \leq c_j = c_j \cdot y_j$.

If no items were packed into b_j, then $y_j = 0$. Additionally, for each item o_i, $x_{i,j} = 0$. Thus, $\sum_{i|b_j \in B_i} x_{i,j} = 0 = c_j \cdot y_j$. Consequently, each constraint of the form $\sum_{i|b_j \in B_i} x_{i,j} \leq c_j \cdot y_j$ in $\mathbf{I_{BMP}}$ is satisfied. Thus, every constraint in $\mathbf{I_{BMP}}$ is satisfied by $(\mathbf{x}, \mathbf{y})$.

For each bin b_j, $y_j = 1$, if and only if P packs an item into b_j. Thus, $\sum_{i=j}^{m} y_j = b^*$. Consequently, $\mathbf{I_{BMP}}$ has a feasible assignment with objective value b^*.

Now assume that $\mathbf{I_{BMP}}$ has a feasible assignment $(\mathbf{x}, \mathbf{y})$ with objective value b^*. From this assignment we construct a packing P of $\mathbf{P}$ as follows: For each item o_i, let $b_j \in B_i$ be a bin such that $x_{i,j} = 1$ (if one exists). Set $P(o_i) = b_j$.

Consider an item o_i. From the constraint $\sum_{b_j \in B_i} x_{i,j} = 1$, we have that $x_{i,j} = 1$ for exactly one bin $b_j \in B_i$ and $x_{i,j'} = 0$ for all $j' \neq j$. Thus, $P(o_i)$ is defined for each item o_i. Consequently, P packs every item in $\mathbf{P}$.

Consider a bin b_j. If $y_j = 1$, then from the constraint $\sum_{i|b_j \in B_i} x_{i,j} \leq c_j \cdot y_j$, we have that $\sum_{i|b_j \in B_i} x_{i,j} \leq c_j$. Thus, there are at most c_j items such that $x_{i,j} = 1$. Consequently, P packs at most c_j items into bin b_j. Since the objective is to minimize $\sum_{i=j}^{m} y_j$, $\sum_{i|b_j \in B_i} x_{i,j} \geq 1$. Otherwise, this constraint (the only constraint to use y_j) could have been satisfied by setting $y_j = 0$. Thus, at least one item is packed into bin b_j.

If $y_j = 0$, then from the constraint $\sum_{i|b_j \in B_i} x_{i,j} \leq c_j \cdot y_j$, we have that $\sum_{i|b_j \in B_i} x_{i,j} = 0$. Thus, no items are packed into bin b_j. Consequently, $y_j = 1$, if and only if an item was packed into bin b_j.

For each bin b_j, P packs item into b_j, if and only if $y_j = 1$. Recall that, $b^* = \sum_{j=1}^{m} y_j$. Consequently, P uses b^* bins. $\qquad\square$

4.1 Cuts

From Sect. 4, BMP for a PBBP-SC instance $\mathbf{P}$ with n items and m bins can be modeled using the IP in System (1).

$$
\begin{aligned}
\min \sum y_j & \\
\sum_{b_j \in B_i} x_{i,j} = 1 \quad & i = 1 \ldots n \\
\sum_{i|b_j \in B_i} x_{i,j} \leq c_j \cdot y_j \quad & j = 1 \ldots m \qquad (1)\\
x_{i,j} \in \{0,1\} \quad & i = 1 \ldots n, \, j = 1 \ldots m \\
y_j \in \{0,1\} \quad & j = 1 \ldots m
\end{aligned}
$$

We will now describe several new forms of constraint that can be added to System (1) to strengthen this formulation.

Let $S \subseteq B$ be a set of bins. We define the following functions of S:

1. $c(S) = \sum_{b_j \in S} c_j$ is the total capacity of the bins in S.
2. $I(S) = |\{o_i : B_i \cap S = \emptyset\}|$ is the number of items which cannot be packed into the bins in S.

For each item o_i and each bin $b_j \in B_i$, we can add the following cut to System (1):

1.) $x_{i,j} \leq y_j$. If item o_i is packed into bin b_j, then b_j is used. We refer to this as an **item-bin cut**.

For each item o_i, we can add the following cut to System (1):

2.) $\sum_{b_j \in B_i} y_j \geq 1$. Item o_i has to be packed into a bin in B_i. Thus, every valid packing needs to use at least one bin in B_i. We refer to this as an **item-subset cut**.

Example 1. Let **P** the following PBBP-SC instance:

1. $B = \{b_1, b_2\}$ where $c_1 = c_2 = 2$. $O = \{o_1, o_2, o_3\}$ where $B_1 = \{b_1\}$, $B_2 = \{b_1, b_2\}$, and $B_3 = \{b_2\}$.

BMP for **P** has the following IP representation:

$$\min \sum y_j$$
$$x_{1,1} = 1$$
$$x_{2,1} + x_{2,2} = 1$$
$$x_{3,2} = 1$$
$$x_{1,1} + x_{2,1} \leq 2 \cdot y_1$$
$$x_{2,2} + x_{3,2} \leq 2 \cdot y_1$$
$$x_{1,1}, x_{2,1}, x_{2,2}, x_{3,2} \in \{0,1\}$$
$$y_1, y_2 \in \{0,1\}$$

If we ignore the restriction to integers, then $(y_1, y_2, x_{1,1}, x_{2,1}, x_{2,2}, x_{3,2}) = (0.75, 0.75, 1, 0.5, 0.5, 1)$ is a valid fractional solution to this formulation. For item o_1, we generate the item-subset cut $y_1 \geq 1$. For item o_3, we generate the item-subset cut $y_2 \geq 1$. These cuts make the optimum solution $(y_1, y_2, x_{1,1}, x_{2,1}, x_{2,2}, x_{3,2}) = (1, 1, 1, 1, 0, 1)$.

For each set O_S of items, we can add the following cut to System (1):

3.) $\sum_{b_j \in \bigcup_{o_i \in O_S} B_i} c_j \cdot y_j \geq |O_S|$. This ensures that for each subset of items, the total capacity of the used bins which can pack the items is enough to pack all of those items. We refer to this as an **item-capacity cut**.

For each set S of bins, we can add the following cuts to System (1):

4.) If $c(S) \leq n$, add the constraint $\sum_{b_j \notin S} y_j \geq 1$. In this case, the bins in S do not have enough capacity to contain all of the items. Thus, every valid packing needs to use at least one bin not in S. We refer to this as a **bin-capacity cut**.

In the above example, if $S = \{b_1\}$, then $c(S) = 2 < 3 = n$. Thus, we generate the capacity cut $y_2 \geq 1$. This is enough to cut out the fractional optimum as a valid solution.

5.) If $I(S) \geq 1$, add the constraint $\sum_{b_j \notin S} y_j \geq 1$. In this case, there exists an item o_i which cannot be packed into any bin in S without violating a subset constraint. Thus, every valid packing needs to use at least one bin not in S. We refer to this as a **bin-subset cut**. For each item o_i, if we choose $S = B \setminus B_i$, then the bin-subset cut for S is the item-subset cut for o_i.

In the above example, if $S = \{b_1\}$, then $I(S) = |\{o_3\}| = 1$. Thus, we generate the bin-subset cut $y_2 \geq 1$. This is enough to cut out the fractional optimum as a valid solution.

6.) Consider the PBBP-SC instance $\mathbf{P}'$ with set of items O and set of bins S. If there is no feasible packing for $\mathbf{P}'$, add the constraint $\sum_{b_j \notin S} y_j \geq 1$. In this case, there is no way to pack all of the items in O into the bins in S. Thus, every valid packing needs to use at least one bin not in S. We refer to this as a **packing cut**.

Note that every capacity cut and bin-subset cut is a packing cut. However, generating a packing cut is more computationally expensive than generating either a capacity or bin-subset cut.

For the PBBP-SC instance $\mathbf{P}$, there are n item-subset cuts, at most 2^m capacity cuts, at most 2^m bin-subset cuts, and at most 2^m packing cuts. Thus, it is straightforward to generate all of the item-subset cuts for $\mathbf{P}$ but computationally expensive to generate all of the capacity, bin-subset, or packing cuts.

In the case of packing cuts, generating all of the packing cuts is equivalent to solving BMP outright. Thus, generating all of the packing cuts makes the IP formulation unnecessary.

5   Experiments

Experiments were executed to compare the average runtimes of solving the BMP problem with each cut type proposed (including no cuts). These experiments were run on an Intel(R) Xeon(R) Gold 6126 CPU at 2.60 GHz with 120 GB memory running Red Hat Enterprise Linux Server 7.9 (Maipo).

Connectivity is selected uniformly at random, selecting numConnections for each item. We consider number of items n to be $100, 200, 300, 400$, number of bins m to be $\log n, \sqrt{n}, n/10$, capacities c to be $n/2$ or n/m. For choosing the subset S, we uniformly randomly sample $m' = n/c$ number of bins, each one is drawn uniformly at random from $[m]$ until $|S| = m$. Subsets of at most $n - 1$ items in O are chosen uniformly at random from the set $[n]$ until $|O| = n$. For $I(S)$, we randomly choose subsets of at most $m - 1$ bins until $|I(S)| = m$.

Results can be seen in Figs. 1, 2, and 3 for the cases where the number of bins m is $\log n, \sqrt{n}$, and $n/10$. Spikes in some of the curves are due to the inherent stochasticity of random problem generation and the empirical complexity of solving integer linear programs for certain problem formulations.

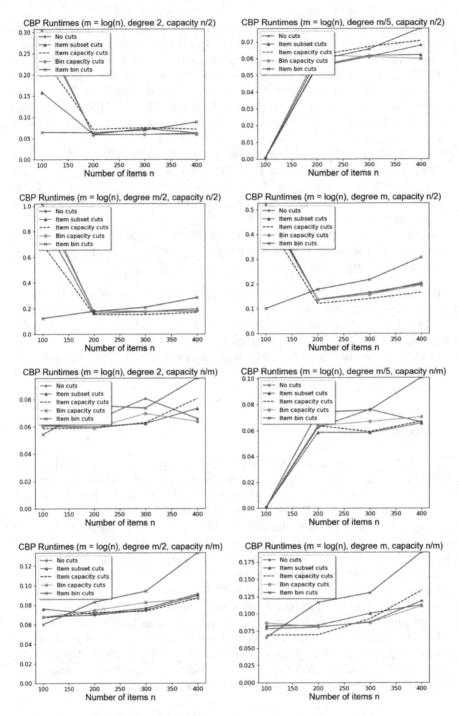

Fig. 1. Average runtimes (in seconds) over at least 100 random instances for each curve, where the number of bins $m = \log n$ for the given number of items n.

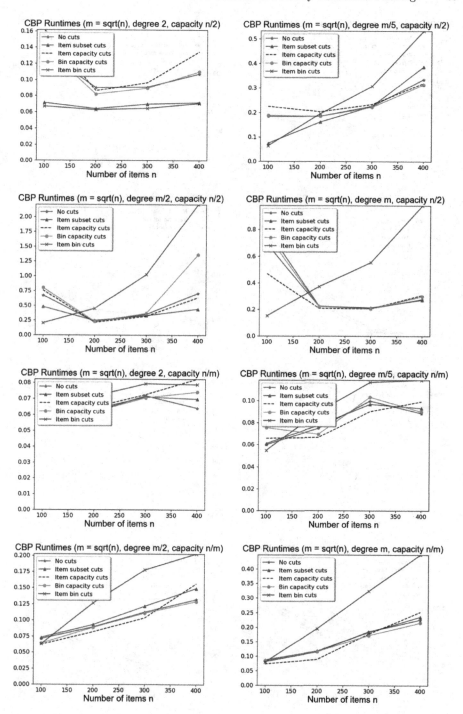

Fig. 2. Average runtimes (in seconds) over at least 100 random instances for each curve, where the number of bins $m = \sqrt{n}$ for the given number of items n.

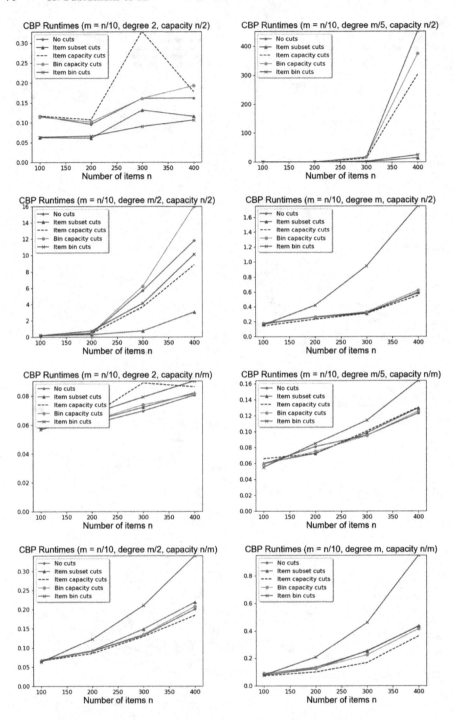

Fig. 3. Average runtimes (in seconds) over at least 100 random instances for each curve, where the number of bins $m = n/10$ for the given number of items n.

6 Conclusion

This paper focused on fine-grained complexity results for variants of the Priority-based bin packing problem with subset constraints. In the case of the bin minimization variant, we showed **W[2]-completeness** when the parameter is the minimum number of bins used and **paraNP-completeness** when the parameter is the maximum number of items that can be packed into any bin. Finally, we provided a detailed empirical analysis of the integer programming models associated with the BMP problem. In this process, several non-trivial cuts with various efficacies were designed. From our perspective, a more detailed empirical analysis would be worthwhile.

References

1. Acikalin, U.U., Caskurlu, B., Wojciechowski, P., Subramani, K.: New results on test-cost minimization in database migration. In: D'Angelo, G., Michail, O. (eds.) ALGOCLOUD 2021. LNCS, vol. 13084, pp. 38–55. Springer, Cham (2021). https://doi.org/10.1007/978-3-030-93043-1_3
2. Ballew, B.: The distributor's three-dimensional pallet-packing problem: a mathematical formulation and heuristic solution approach. Master's thesis, Air Force Institute of Technology, March 2000
3. Borradaile, G., Heeringa, B., Wilfong, G.T.: The knapsack problem with neighbour constraints. J. Discrete Algorithms **16**, 224–235 (2012)
4. Bringmann, K.: Fine-grained complexity theory (tutorial). In Rolf Niedermeier and Christophe Paul, editors, 36th International Symposium on Theoretical Aspects of Computer Science, STACS 2019, March 13–16, 2019, Berlin, Germany, vol. 126 of LIPIcs, pp. 4:1–4:7. Schloss Dagstuhl - Leibniz-Zentrum für Informatik (2019)
5. Brodal, G.S., Frigioni, D., Marchetti-Spaccamela, A. (eds.): WAE 2001. LNCS, vol. 2141. Springer, Heidelberg (2001). https://doi.org/10.1007/3-540-44688-5
6. Cygan, M., Fomin, F.V., Kowalik, Ł, Lokshtanov, D., Marx, D., Pilipczuk, M., Pilipczuk, M., Saurabh, S.: Parameterized Algorithms. Springer, Cham (2015). https://doi.org/10.1007/978-3-319-21275-3
7. Drumm, C., Schmitt, M., Do, H.H., Rahm, E.: Quickmig: automatic schema matching for data migration projects. In: Proceedings of the Sixteenth ACM Conference on Information and Knowledge Management, CIKM 2007, Lisbon, Portugal, 6–10 November 2007, pp. 107–116 (2007)
8. Fomin, F.V., Lokshtanov, D., Saurabh, S., Zehavi, M.: Theory of Parameterized Preprocessing. Cambridge University Press, Kernelization (2019)
9. Gandhi, R., Halldórsson, M.M., Kortsarz, G., Shachnai, H.: Improved results for data migration and open shop scheduling. In: Díaz, J., Karhumäki, J., Lepistö, A., Sannella, D. (eds.) ICALP 2004. LNCS, vol. 3142, pp. 658–669. Springer, Heidelberg (2004). https://doi.org/10.1007/978-3-540-27836-8_56
10. Garey, M.R., Johnson, D.S.: Computers and Intractability: A Guide to the Theory of NP-Completeness. W. H. Freeman Company, San Francisco (1979)
11. Goldman, R., McHugh, J., Widom, J.: From semistructured data to XML: migrating the lore data model and query language. In: ACM SIGMOD Workshop on The Web and Databases, WebDB 1999, Philadelphia, Pennsylvania, USA, 3–4 June 1999. Informal Proceedings, pp. 25–30 (1999)

12. Golubchik, L., Khuller, S., Kim, Y.A., Shargorodskaya, S., (Justin) Wan, Y.-C.: Data migration on parallel disks. In: Algorithms - ESA 2004, 12th Annual European Symposium, Bergen, Norway, 14–17 September 2004, Proceedings, pp. 689–701 (2004)

13. Hall, J., Hartline, J.D., Karlin, A.R., Saia, J., Wilkes, J.: On algorithms for efficient data migration. In: Proceedings of the Twelfth Annual Symposium on Discrete Algorithms, 7–9 January 2001, Washington, DC, USA, pp. 620–629 (2001)

14. Hodgson, T.J.: A combined approach to the pallet loading problem. A I I E Transactions **14**(3), 175–182 (1982)

15. Jansen, K., Kratsch, S., Marx, D., Schlotter, I.: Bin packing with fixed number of bins revisited. J. Comput. Syst. Sci. **79**(1), 39–49 (2013)

16. Martello, S., Toth, P.: Knapsack Problems: Algorithms and Computer Implementations. Wiley, Chichester (1990)

17. Martins, G.H.A., Dell, R.F.: Solving the pallet loading problem. Eur. J. Oper. Res. **184**(2), 429–440 (2008)

18. Subramani, K., Caskurlu, B., Acikalin, U.U.: Security-aware database migration planning. In: Brandic, I., Genez, T.A.L., Pietri, I., Sakellariou, R. (eds.) ALGOCLOUD 2019. LNCS, vol. 12041, pp. 103–121. Springer, Cham (2020). https://doi.org/10.1007/978-3-030-58628-7_7

19. Subramani, K., Caskurlu, B., Velasquez, A.: Minimization of testing costs in capacity-constrained database migration. In: Disser, Y., Verykios, V.S. (eds.) ALGOCLOUD 2018. LNCS, vol. 11409, pp. 1–12. Springer, Cham (2019). https://doi.org/10.1007/978-3-030-19759-9_1

20. Tovey, C.A.: A simplified np-complete satisfiability problem. Discret. Appl. Math. **8**(1), 85–89 (1984)

21. Wojciechowski, P., Subramani, K., Velasquez, A., Caskurlu, B.: Algorithmic analysis of priority-based bin packing. In: Mudgal, A., Subramanian, C.R. (eds.) CALDAM 2021. LNCS, vol. 12601, pp. 359–372. Springer, Cham (2021). https://doi.org/10.1007/978-3-030-67899-9_29

More Sparking Soundex-Based Privacy-Preserving Record Linkage

Alexandros Karakasidis[✉] and Georgia Koloniari

Department of Applied Informatics, University of Macedonia, Thessaloniki, Greece
{a.karakasidis,gkoloniari}@uom.edu.gr

Abstract. Privacy preserving record linkage refers to the problem of matching records from two or more data holders without revealing any personal identifiers, thus, maintaining the privacy of the individuals described by these records. While parallel processing has been deployed in the context of privacy preserving record linkage for handling big data, in this paper, we further explore parallel methods based on Apache Spark and phonetic codes and propose improvements, which manage to achieve superior performance with respect to time efficiency and privacy characteristics. To support our claims, we provide extensive experimental results and a rigorous discussion.

Keywords: Big Data · Privacy-Preserving Record Linkage · Soundex

1 Introduction

Contemporary times are characterized by a mix of situations that are unprecedented. We are experiencing a pandemic for the last years, while, at the same time, military conflicts emerge throughout the world contributing to the already existing refugee crisis. These facts lead governments to take action, enforcing strict measures in order to address these issues. As such, there is the need to transfer personal data between organizations and companies for a variety of purposes, ranging from tracing COVID-19 infection cases to identifying refugees. This is, however, not a trivial task. Identifying the same individual across databases of different organizations poses a series of technical, ethical, and as a result of the latter, legal challenges.

Beginning with the technical challenges, as databases originate from different organizations, they do not exhibit the same schemas and may not have common candidate keys. Thus, their records cannot be matched using a common unique identifier and alternative solutions have to be examined. To this end, combinations of fields, usually consisting of strings, that contain personal information may be used to uniquely identify an individual across different databases. Such fields are called quasi-identifiers and the problem in this case is that they are error-prone, since they are usually the result of manual input.

What we have just described is the traditional record linkage problem, pertaining more than a century, when Soundex [20], a phonetic encoding scheme that

L. Foschini and S. Kontogiannis (Eds.): ALGOCLOUD 2022, LNCS 13799, pp. 73–93, 2023.
https://doi.org/10.1007/978-3-031-33437-5_5

matches similarly sounding names, was created for this purpose. Record linkage is an inherently complicated problem. Considering the case of two data holders, all their records have to be compared. Furthermore, the use of approximate matching techniques, to handle errors in data, usually increases computational complexity. This, however, does not occur with Soundex, as it is a generalization technique with the capacity of absorbing errors and, as such, its output is suitable for exact matching.

Nowadays, there are additional complications that make solving this task even more challenging. First of all, the volumes of data that have to be processed has increased to extents that single computers may not suffice for this purpose. To this end, big data processing frameworks have been employed so as to distribute computation among multiple computers. On top of that, ethical and legal concerns regarding personal data processing are raised by modern legislation as GDPR and HIPAA. Consequently, data may not be transferred as free text between organizations, as such an action would reveal personal information, uniquely identifying individuals using the quasi-identifiers described earlier. This leads us to seek techniques that will allow as to perform record linkage without harming the privacy of these individuals.

This is the privacy-preserving version of the record linkage problem. In privacy-preserving record linkage we aim at identifying the same real world entity, e.g. a person, among distinct data holders, also requiring that these data holders gain no additional knowledge apart from the matching entities and no information regarding all entities in the datasets should be further disclosed.

In this paper, we build upon the Parallel Soundex method [12] which relies on Apache Spark. The main points of this method are the following. Soundex is used as an approximate string matching operator. Privacy is preserved through a combination of measures. First, Soundex inherent generalization properties are exploited, as more than one strings map to the same Soundex code. Then, each of these codes is encoded by a secure hash function. The next measure taken is noise injection, so as to shuffle original records with fake ones rendering them indistinguishable. Finally, a third matching party is employed so as to mediate between data holders. This third party leverages the benefits of secure multiparty computation, where multiple parties cooperate to perform a calculation with each of them having access only to a part of the required data.

In our work, we make the following contributions. First, we provide speedups to Parallel Soundex of more than 3. Second, we achieve superior privacy characteristics. For this purpose, we propose two methods: Parallel Soundex, Partition-wise Shuffling (PSPS) and Parallel Soundex, Partition-wise Shuffling, Single Hash (PSPSSH). PSPS speeds up Spark-based computation of arbitrary sized datasets, while PSPSSH achieves even further speedups and improved privacy characteristics, given certain constraints in the dataset and noise sizes.

The rest of this paper is organized as follows. In Sect. 2, we provide the necessary background to deploy our approach. The methodology we follow is laid in Sect. 3, while Sect. 4 includes a detailed privacy analysis of our methods. Section 5 holds the experimental evaluation of our proposed approaches. In Sect. 6, we present works related to ours, and we conclude in Sect. 7.

2   Problem Formulation and Background

In this section, we formally define the problem we are solving and provide the necessary background for laying out our solution.

2.1   Problem Formulation

Without loss of generality, let us consider two data sources, called Alice (A) and Bob (B), who respectively hold r^A and r^B records each. We denote as r_i^A and r_i^B the i-th record of Alice and Bob, respectively. We represent the j-th attribute of these records as $r_i^A.j$ and $r_i^B.j$.

Privacy preserving record linkage is the problem of identifying (linking) all pairs of r^A and r^B records that refer to the same real world entity, so that no more information is disclosed to either A, B or any third party involved in the process besides the identifiers of the linked r^As and r^Bs.

Presumably, Alice and Bob use different schemas in their databases. As such, their records have different attributes and share no common candidate key. Let R^A be Alice's schema and R^B be Bob's schema and let us assume that in these schemas m of the attributes are common between the two sources forming a composite key. These attributes are quasi-identifiers and might consist of names, surnames, addresses, birth dates. As such, none of these on its own can be used to identify a record. We refer to these attributes as *matching attributes* or *matching fields*. The composite key is used to determine when two records *match*, i.e., when they refer to the same entity, by comparing the respective attributes. Considering that our data is often dirty, matching should rely on a similarity or distance function.

Let us consider $\mathcal{D}$ as the domain of each matching attribute, a similarity function $sim_j() : \mathcal{D} \times \mathcal{D} \rightarrow [0..1]$ and a threshold $t_j > 0$. Given records r_i^A and r_i^B with matching attributes $r_i.1, \ldots, r_i.m$ for both Alice and Bob, we define the following matching function $M : \mathcal{D} \times \mathcal{D} \rightarrow \{0, 1\}$:

$$M(r_i^A, r_i^B) = \begin{cases} 1, & \text{iff } sim_j(r_i^A.j, r_i^B.j) \geq t_j, \forall j \in [1, m] \\ 0, & \text{otherwise.} \end{cases} \tag{1}$$

If $M(r_i^A, r_i^B) = 1$, then the pair (r_i^A, r_i^B) is a match.

This process is the *matching process*. To preserve privacy, i.e., ensure *privacy preserving matching* (PPM), after the completion of this process, the only information revealed is the identifiers of the matched records.

Table 1. Soundex conversion table.

a, e, h, i, o, u, w, y	→ 0	l	→ 4
b, f, p, v	→ 1	m, n	→ 5
c, g, j, k, q, s, x, z	→ 2	r	→ 6
d, t	→ 3		

2.2 Phonetic Algorithms for String Matching

Equation 1 is applicable to any attribute type. However, the majority of quasi-identifiers used to compare records in the context of linking sensitive databases contain textual values [4]. Thus, in this work, we focus on string matching attributes, e.g. names, addresses, that offer identifying information for individuals. For numerical fields, matching methods such as [24] may be used.

A phonetic algorithm is a method for mapping a word to its pronunciation. Such algorithms have been widely used in the past when performing record matching on names. Their key feature is that they can achieve fault tolerance against spelling errors through clustering similar sounding letters and suppressing information as multiple names may map to the same code. Using phonetic algorithms for matching may be formalized via Eq. 1. The formula's similarity function sim_j will have as input two phonetic codes and examine if these match, returning 1, when the two codes are identical and 0, otherwise. As such, the matching threshold t_j is set to 1.

2.3 The Soundex Algorithm

Soundex, based on English language pronunciation, is the oldest (patented in 1918 [20]) and one of the most popular phonetic encoding algorithms. Soundex maintains the first letter of a string, commonly a name, and converts the rest into numbers, using predefined mappings shown in Table 1. All zeros (vowels, 'h', 'w' and 'y') are then removed and sequences of the same number are merged to a single one (e.g. '44' is replaced with '4'). The final code is the original first letter and three numbers. Longer codes are stripped off, while shorter codes are padded with zeros.

Now, let us get some insights on Soundex operation. Soundex for either SMITH or SMYTH yields S530. The same occurs for BAGBY and BISCHOFF, with B210. Most probably the first pair of surnames is a misspelling and the fact that Soundex results in the same encoding indicates its error absorbing capacity. On the other hand, the second pair of surnames are undoubtedly different. Yet, Soundex yields the same code, which indicates its generalization property.

2.4 Apache Spark

Apache Spark [33] is an open source, memory-based framework, designed for big data processing. It is considered state-of-the-art, overtaking Hadoop MapReduce. Spark performs better in many ways [29]: it is faster, easier to program, and it goes far beyond batch applications to support a variety of compute-intensive tasks. Also, it supports rich APIs in several languages (Scala, Java, Python, SQL and R) for performing complex operations on distributed data. Furthermore, Spark's memory model, leverages the use of main memory, thus outperforming Hadoop's MapReduce [26].

Its design is based on a data abstraction called Resilient Distributed Dataset (RDD). Users create RDDs by defining *transformations* to their data. Transformations return new RDD objects representing the result of computations. But computations do not take place immediately, but only after specific commands called *actions* are defined. Thus, Spark is coined to follow *lazy evaluation*.

A Spark cluster comprises of a set of key entities [26]. The *driver* is a program that considers Spark as a library and describes the computation operations to be performed. The workers provide resources to the Spark application, namely CPU, memory and storage, hosting *executors* which are distinct Java Virtual Machine processes that perform computation. A set of computations is referred to as a job. This is launched in a cluster by Spark and concludes with the results, which are returned to the driver program. A Spark application may consist of multiple jobs. Each time a job is provided to Spark, it forms a directed acyclic graph of stages. Each stage, in its turn is a collection of tasks, each of which comprises the smallest unit of work that Spark sends to an executor. To enable parallel processing by executors, RDDs are partitioned into chunks across the cluster. These partitions are the in-memory equivalents of Hadoop HDFS blocks, where data are usually stored in such setups, while they can also be created at runtime by the driver. Some transformations are applied within each partition, named *narrow* transformations, while others require data exchanges among partitions, and as a result, workers, named wide transformations. The latter lead to data shuffles and network traffic between nodes.

3 Methodology

In this section, we first describe Parallel Soundex (PS) as introduced in [12]. Then, we present two enhancements. The first one, called Parallel Soundex Partition-wise Shuffle (PSPS) performs per-partition shuffling. The second one, called Parallel Soundex Partition-wise Shuffle with Single Hash (PSPSSH) builds upon PSPS and reduces execution time while improving privacy.

3.1 Parallel Soundex

In Sect. 2, we illustrated two properties of Soundex. The first one is that it manages to absorb misspellings. This shifts the approximate string matching problem to exact Soundex matching. The second one is that it manages to act as a generalization mechanism. Based on these properties, we will now describe a protocol for parallel privacy-preserving record linkage.

In this protocol, we assume two data holders, named Alice and Bob, and a third party called Carol who will mediate between them for the privacy-preserving matching process. We further assume that all three parties are operating their own Spark clusters for data processing. Initially, Alice and Bob agree on a set of common fields in their schemas to be used as matching fields. As Alice and Bob's data do not have to conform to the exact same schema and usually exhibit heterogeneity, to privately determine matching attributes, privacy preserving schema matching algorithms [5,27] may be deployed.

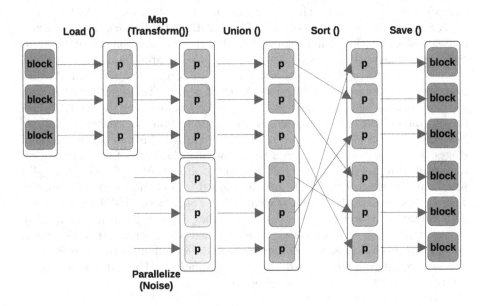

Fig. 1. PS workflow at Alice and Bob.

Each of the data holders performs for each matching field of each row a *Map* operation which performs the following narrow transformations: $Data \longrightarrow Soundex\_Code \longrightarrow Hash$ resulting in an RDD with hash codes. A map operation is also performed so as to generate an RDD with random noise. The transformations in this case are: $Random\_Soundex\_Code \longrightarrow Hash$. This can be done according to [15] where k-anonymity is ensured. Then, a union operation between these two RDDs takes place and the rows of the resulting RDD are randomly ordered by performing an $orderBy(random)$ operation. This results in globally shuffling all records within all RDD partitions in the cluster. This step concludes data preparation for Alice and Bob. The entire process is illustrated in Fig. 1.

Next, as illustrated in Fig. 2(A), Alice and Bob deliver the resulting datasets, through a secure channel, to Carol. Carol, upon receiving the datasets, transforms them into RDDs to perform the join operation in her Spark cluster. Each party's records participating in the resulting RDD are then securely delivered to Alice and Bob (Fig. 2(B)) respectively, who independently join the received records with their own datasets to phase out noise and eventually securely deliver matching records to each other (Fig. 2(C)).

3.2   Parallel Soundex, Partition-Wise Shuffling

To maintain privacy in PS, original data has to be mixed with generated noise and shuffled. Nevertheless, this comes at a cost. In contrast with the sequential case, data to be sorted are dispersed in different workers. As a result, for a Spark orderBy operation to take place, data shuffle between partitions, usually residing within different workers, has to take place. Moving data between workers is not the most efficient way to go.

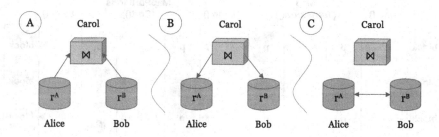

Fig. 2. Overview of the phonetic matching protocol.

To address this issue, we consider the following alternative, as illustrated in Fig. 3. Instead of shuffling in a cluster-wide manner the entire dataset, we perform partition-wise shuffling. In this case, data are shuffled locally, per-partition, avoiding data transfers among workers. This is expected to decrease overall transformation time at Alice and Bob. However, shuffling is a crucial step for the privacy of the method making noise and real records indistinguishable. The question rising here is how partition-wise shuffling affects privacy. To answer this, we rely on Lemma 1 to calculate the probabilities of randomly identifying a true tuple of the dataset. Let us consider a dataset D of size equal to $|D|$ that is dispersed within $|P|$ partitions. Let us also consider a noise multiplication factor N which designates the amount of additional noise injected.

Lemma 1. *The probability P_{PS} of randomly selecting a real record using Parallel Soundex is equal to the probability P_{PSPS} of randomly selecting a real record using Parallel Soundex, Partition-wise Shuffling.*

Proof. For the case of PS, the encoded dataset D_{ENC} size is $|D_{ENC}| = |D| + N \cdot |D| = (N+1) \cdot |D|$. As such, the probability of randomly selecting a real record is equal to $P_{PS} = \frac{|D|}{|D_{ENC}|} = \frac{|D|}{(N+1) \cdot |D|} = \frac{1}{(N+1)}$.

Now, for the case of PSPS, we consider that D is divided into $|P|$ partitions. Similarly, for each partition, after noise injection, $|D_{ENC}| = \frac{|D|}{|P|} + N \cdot \frac{|D|}{|P|} =$

$(N + 1) \cdot \frac{|D|}{|P|}$. The probability of randomly selecting a real record in one of the $|P|$ partitions is $P_{PSPS} = \frac{\frac{|D|}{|P|}}{(N+1) \cdot \frac{|D|}{|P|}} = \frac{\frac{|D|}{|P|}}{(N+1) \cdot \frac{|D|}{|P|}} = \frac{1}{(N+1)}$.

3.3   Parallel Soundex, Partition-Wise Shuffling, Single Hash

PSPS offers an enhancement to PS exploiting the capabilities of the Spark framework. Now, we will move a step further and describe an alteration to the protocol, also applicable to the sequential approach presented in [14]. We call this enhancement Parallel Soundex, Partition-wise Shuffling, Single Hash (PSPSSH).

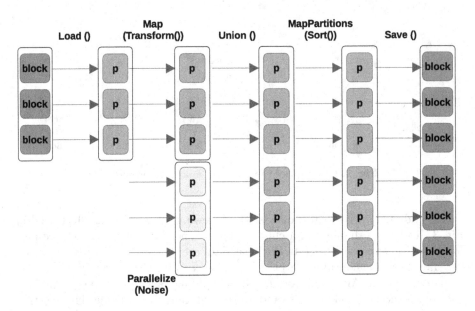

Fig. 3. PSPS/PSPSSH workflow at Alice and Bob.

In PS and PSPS, each field is transformed to its Soundex equivalent and then it is hashed through a secure hash function to create a ciphertext, as shown on the left branch of Fig. 4. This way, the number of ciphertexts created is equal to the number of matching fields. In PSPSSH, we propose concatenating all Soundex encodings of a record's matching fields, and hashing the entire concatenation resulting in a single ciphertext, as illustrated on the right branch of Fig. 4. This approach has the following benefits. First, hashing occurs only once, instead of hashing equal times to the number of m matching fields. This also reduces the number of transferred hashes over the network by a factor of m. This reduction in the workload also holds for Carol, who performs join on a single field instead of m. These benefits can be exploited under the limitations outlined in Lemma 2.

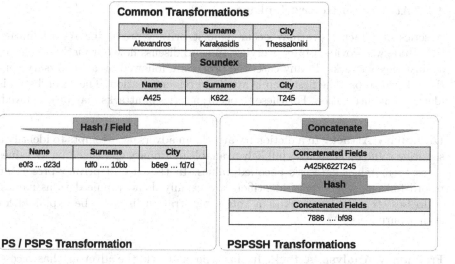

Fig. 4. Transformations at Alice and Bob.

Lemma 2. *Given a dataset of size $|D|$ where N times noise is added and a uniform secure hash function of b bits, PSPSSH may be used when $(1 + N) \cdot |D| < 2^b$.*

Proof. Using PSPSSH, a single ciphertext for all matching fields per record is used, resulting into $|D|$ ciphertexts. Adding noise equal to N times the dataset size results into $|D| + N \cdot |D| = (1 + N) \cdot |D|$ records. These should be encoded without collisions by the hash function. As such, $(1 + N) \cdot |D| < 2^b$.

In terms of privacy, as the noise generation method and record shuffling in PSPSSH are the same with PSPS, Lemma 1 also holds for PSPSSH. However, PSPSSH comes with enhanced privacy characteristics. These stem from the fact that all Soundex codes are concatenated before being hashed into a single field. As such, even in the case that an adversary recovers a real record, they will have to overcome a series of problems in order to succeed in a brute force attack. First of all, the attacker will not know the number of matching fields encoded within the hash. As such, they will have to guess the number of fields used, thus increasing the time required for the attack. Even in the case that they manage to identify the number of fields used, they will not be aware of the order that these fields have been concatenated.

4   Privacy Analysis

In this section, we provide a rigorous privacy analysis of our protocol, focusing on the PSPSSH approach to showcase its enhanced privacy characteristics. First, we lay out a brief description of possible attacks against privacy-preserving record linkage. Then, we prove the resilience of our protocol, considering the participating entities, the data holders (Alice and Bob) and the third party (Carol).

4.1   Attacks on Record Linkage

A series of attack types may occur against privacy-preserving record linkage [32]. Here, we provide a brief overview so as to discuss how our method behaves against these attacks. In any case, the procedure followed by an adversary consists of two steps. The first step is attribute reidentification. The second step is identity reidentification. For these to occur, a series of attacks may be employed.

Dictionary Attack. In a dictionary attack, an adversary attempts to identify a sensitive value by utilizing a publicly available dictionary and encoding its values so as to match a dataset's encoded values. In the case of privacy-preserving record linkage, where quasi-identifiers are usually demographic data as names, addresses etc., a phonebook or a voters registration list may be exploited for such a purpose.

Frequency Analysis Attack. In this type of attack, the adversary has access, as in the previous case, to a publicly available plain text dataset. They then study the distribution of this dataset and compare it with the attribute distributions of the encoded dataset so as to identify quasi-identifier attributes.

Similarity Attacks. According to Eq. 1 of the privacy-preserving matching definition, matching is performed using similarity thresholds over encoded fields. Similarity attacks are based on the fact that distributions of similarities between encoded and plain text fields are maintained. Thus, an adversary may exploit this observation so as to relate plain text values with encoded values.

Linkage and Ciphertext-only Attacks. These attacks are not directly related to privacy-preserving record linkage but rather with privacy-preserving data publishing. The core of the Linkage attack relies on linking publicly available information so as to reveal due to the uniqueness of these values, the quasi-identifiers. Such an attack may be facilitated under collusion between a data holder and a third party. Nevertheless, such attacks have not been reported [32]. In Ciphertext-only attacks, the adversary analyses ciphertexts to recover plain texts. However, this is not usual in privacy-preserving record linkage, as certain values may change over the time.

4.2   Behavior Against Attacks

We first prove some of the PSPSSH protocol's properties that we will use to evaluate the method's behavior against the aforementioned attacks. Some of the properties pertain to all our PS-based protocols, i.e., PS, PSPS and PSPSSH, while some apply only to the latter. All properties stem from the fact that all participants in our protocol are Honest but Curious. They will try to infer as much information as possible from the protocol without attacking it, as they would not wish to jeopardize their reputation. We begin our analysis with the case of the data holders and then proceed to Carol. Finally, we examine what information may be leaked to an external attacker.

Proposition 1. *In all PS-based protocols, Alice and Bob gain no further information on each other's dataset beyond matching record identifiers.*

Proof. Alice and Bob have no direct access to each other's data, and they interact with each other directly only after matching has been performed by Carol. In particular, according to step (5) of the PPRL protocol (Sect. 2.3), Alice and Bob exchange their matching rows. Thus, no other data is leaked as defined by the objective of PPRL. The only case of unwanted leakage information here is that of a false positive match.

Carol, on the other hand, has direct access to encrypted data of both data holders. As such, it would be interesting to examine her success on each of the attack types.

Proposition 2. *In PSPSSH, a dictionary attack by Carol, or an external adversary, is equivalent to a Ciphertext-only attack.*

Proof. Carol receives a set of hashes. Each hash contains a padded concatenation of the Soundex-encoded matching attributes in an arbitrary order. For Carol to effectively recover a value, she first has to access the padded value, which, however, is not disclosed to her. Beyond the padding, the encoding is row-wise, as in a single hash all matching attributes are encoded. Thus, a dictionary attack is impossible and Carol has to perform a brute force attack in order to recover any values.

Proposition 3. *In PSPSSH, a frequency attack by Carol, or an external attacker, is equivalent to a Ciphertext-only attack.*

Proof. To perform a successful frequency attack, Carol has to analyze the frequencies of the received hashes. Nevertheless, each of these hashes corresponds to a single record, while all records are deduplicated, thus each of them is unique. Therefore, Carol cannot perform a frequency analysis, neither on a field, nor on an entire record. On top of that, noise is injected, refraining Carol from discerning real from noise records.

Proposition 4. *All PS-based protocols are immune to Similarity attacks.*

Proof. The proposed Soundex-based protocol matching used in all PS-based approaches is not based on similarity thresholds, but on joins, thus being immune to this type of attack, as there are no similarity distributions.

Proposition 5. *PSPSSH is immune to Ciphertext-only attacks.*

Proof. Let us assume that Carol tries a brute-force attack. As noise is used in all PS-based protocols, Carol is not aware of which records correspond to real data, thus having to analyze the entire dataset. Having the entire dataset analyzed, she does not know the matching fields used and particularly for PSPSSH neither their number, nor the order these have been concatenated, thus being without any context. For PS and PSPS, she does know the number of matching fields used, but in any case, she will not succeed in launching a dictionary or frequency attack, neither on a field, nor on an entire record, as noise records exist.

Even if she attempts to perform a linkage attack on a decrypted record, she is not able to know whether this record is real or noise. And as she does not know the context of each of the concatenated fields and their order her confidence will be equal to $\frac{1}{Perm(m)}$, where Perm(m) is the number of permutations of the matching fields. Even in this case, she is not be able to revert to the original plain texts, as Soundex exhibits a generalization mechanism, where a single encoding maps to more than one plain texts.

5   Experiments

In this section, we present experimental evidence supporting the efficiency and efficacy of our approach. Initially, we describe our experimental setup, then we provide experiments regarding matching and time performance.

5.1   Setup

We rely on real world data originating from North Carolina's publicly available voter's database. We determined five matching fields, namely: 'last_name', 'first_name', 'midl_name', 'res_street_address', 'res_city_desc'. The first three fields are self-descriptive. The two last ones hold the person's address and city of residence. As addresses start with a number, we converted all numbers in this field into the corresponding verbals. The database was deduplicated using these fields so that all five of them comprise a candidate key.

To evaluate the scalability of our techniques, we uniformly sampled this database, ending up with three datasets for Alice and Bob of sizes: 800K, 1600K and 3200K records, i.e., for instance, 800K denotes that Alice and Bob hold 800,000 records each. For all sizes, Alice's and Bob's datasets overlap by 25%, i.e., for the 800K one, 200,000 records should be matched. Furthermore, since we focus on approximate matching, Bob's records that match Alice's have been corrupted by randomly choosing a field of each row and randomly performing a character deletion, insertion or transposition with another, so that join operations between Alice's and Bob's data yield zero matching records. Regarding noise, we generate fake records at each data holder as a percentage of the size of the original dataset, each of them consisting of fake Soundex codes. As such, producing 100% noise means that we produce the same number of fake records as the original dataset. In our evaluation, we experiment with 100%, 200%. 400% and 800% of noise.

To conduct our experiments, we have setup a cluster hosted in the cloud by the IaaS service of GRNET[1] consisting of 11 virtual machines, each having 16 GB of RAM and 8 Xeon CPUs at 2.3 GHz. The cluster features distributed storage supported by Apache Hadoop 2 HDFS, while the computation engine is Apache PySpark 2.4.7. One virtual machine has been used as a dedicated master, while the rest of them were operating as workers. We have fixed the driver's memory to 12 GBs, while we have allocated 2 GBs of memory and one core to each executor, totaling to 70 executors. Finally, we have fixed the number of data partitions to 100 so as to exploit the number of available executors.

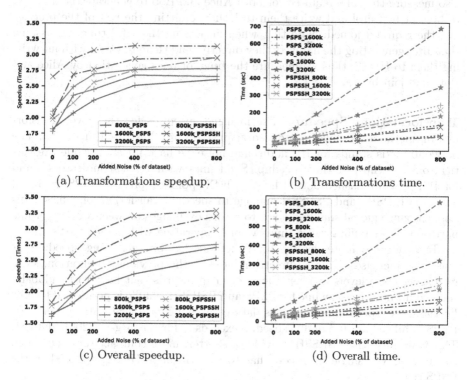

(a) Transformations speedup.

(b) Transformations time.

(c) Overall speedup.

(d) Overall time.

Fig. 5. Results for time performance evaluation.

5.2   Matching Performance

We assess matching performance in terms of F_1-Score, which is a measure of accuracy defined as the harmonic mean of precision and recall: $F_1\text{-}Score = \frac{TP}{TP+0.5(FP+FN)}$. Our evaluation indicates that alterations made on PS had no

---

[1] https://okeanos-knossos.grnet.gr/home/.

practical impact on its matching quality, providing identical results for all three methods, i.e., PS and the improved PSPS and PSPSSH. In all cases, the F_1-Scores remained identical and equal to 0.752, even in the extreme case of injecting noise equal to 800% of the dataset size. These outcomes show that our methods are scalable and their performance remains consistent.

5.3   Time Performance

We evaluate time performance of the alternative methods we propose by measuring elapsed clock time and indicating the incurred speedup of each approach with respect to PS. Besides measuring the overall time of the entire process, to better assess the benefits incurred by the proposed transformation methods, we also measure the time required for both Alice and Bob to generate the datasets to be sent to Carol and write them to HDFS, omitting the rest of the process, i.e., the required joined. Note that when measuring the total time, we assume that after generating the datasets they directly send them to Carol without writing them to HDFS, thus we measure the time for data generation by Alice and Bob, and join by Carol.

Transformations Speedup. The incurred speedups for the novel transformation methods we have introduced against PS are illustrated in Fig. 5a. The horizontal axis stands for the additional noise we have injected, while the vertical one for the resulting speedup. Solid lines with vertical indicators stand for PSPS, while dashed-dotted lines with 'X' points represent PSPSSH. In all cases, both PSPS and PSPSSH manage to speedup transformation times. This happens since global shuffling leads to record exchanges between workers, while partition-wise shuffling saves time by solely operating within each partition.

To delve into more details, both methods exhibit increasing speedups as noise size increases. This is directly related to the previous observation, since increasing noise levels increase the number of records that have to be globally shuffled in the PS case, while for PSPS and PSPSSH, shuffle is performed locally. Furthermore, speedup increases as dataset sizes increase. PSPSSH outperforms PSPS in all cases. Marginally, speedup exceeds 3, for the largest 3200K dataset. This is because the PSPSSH provides a shorter, more compact representation. As such, only a single hash code has to be written to HDFS, opposed to the PSPS case.

Elapsed clock times are illustrated in Fig. 5b. The horizontal axis stands again for the percentages of additional noise injected, while the vertical one represents elapsed time in seconds. Dashed lines with star points illustrate PS behavior, dotted lines with crosses are for PSPS, while dashed-dotted lines with 'X' points are for PSPSSH. Here, we observe the linear time behavior of the dataset transformations for PS; when doubling the added noise, processing time doubles. For PSPS and especially for PSPSSH this behavior becomes sublinear, as the slopes are less steep. Here, doubling the noise injected increases transformation time by a factor less than two.

Overall Speedup. Let us now examine the overall speedup achieved, i.e., including join time by Carol as well. As illustrated in Fig. 5c, the behavior is similar with the one exhibited in Fig. 5a. This is expected, as the only differences with the previous set of experiments is that Alice and Bob's transformations are not written to HDFS but immediately joined. This is the reason for the lower overall times illustrated in Fig. 5d compared to Fig. 5b. However, we observe in Fig. 5c that for PSPSSH, speedup is further elevated reaching 3.25. This occurs for the following two reasons. First, with PSPSSH's compact representation, less data have to be transferred across the network. Second, joins require less time. For PSPSSH joins are reduced to comparing a single field, as opposed to PS and PSPS that involve multiple fields (here, five fields).

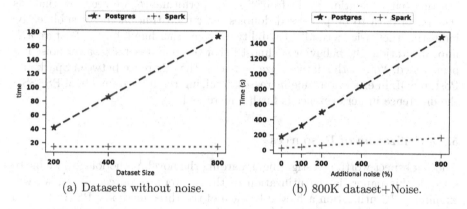

(a) Datasets without noise.   (b) 800K dataset+Noise.

Fig. 6. Comparison with Postgres.

Comparison with RDBMS. We also employ PostgreSQL for comparison. Alice and Bob's data are retrieved, encoded and then stored into separate tables. For Carol to perform her joins, an index is built on matching attributes.

Let us now compare the performance of our initial PS implementation in Spark to that of PostgreSQL, so as to examine the benefits of a parallel architecture. There are two aspects in our comparison. First, we examine how these two methods compare when no noise is employed for various dataset sizes, and then, we keep the size of the dataset fixed and compare how the two implementations behave in terms of noise addition. Time, in all cases, represents the time required to read the initial datasets, transform them, join them and count the number of joinned records.

Let us begin with the case where no noise is added, as illustrated in Fig. 6a. Here, we have used smaller datasets, as the processing capacity of the RDBMS is expected to be inferior of that of the clustered Spark implementation. The horizontal axis of the plot stands for the dataset size employed, while the vertical one for the overall elapsed time in seconds. As we can see, Spark's time performance remains practically unchanged, regardless of the increase in the size of the dataset. This indicates two things. First, that our cluster's capacity exceeds the processing power required for these datasets. Second, that even in the basic implementation of PS, the utilization of cluster resources is according to the corresponding workload. With regard to the implementation of PostgreSQL, we observe that, thanks to the indexes used for matching, the behavior of this method is almost linear. Yet, as the size of the dataset increases, processing time is more than doubled.

Moving on to Fig. 6b, we have illustrated the processing time required for both engines, PostgreSQL and Apache Spark, when adding noise to the 800K dataset. As such, in this case, the X axis represents the percentage of noise added to the initial dataset, while the Y axis represents, again elapsed time. Starting our evaluation again from Spark's performance, we see here that, as the size of data to be processed doubles, execution time increases sublinearly, indicating the basic method's scalability. On the other hand, for the PostgreSQL implementation, the behavior is almost linear to the dataset size, after noise has been added. Yet, as the dataset size increases, the difference between Spark and PostgreSQL in execution time increases. Utilizing the improvements of PSPSSH the difference in performance is further increased.

5.4   Utilization of Resources

Another aspect worth investigating, regarding the novel methodologies we intro-duce in this paper, is the utilization of the cluster's resources. First, we will examine CPU utilization achieved by each of the three methods: PS, PSPS and PSPSSH. To proceed with this evaluation, we have employed Delight[2], and relied on its Efficiency Ratio metric which is defined in Delight's manual as "The ratio of Spark tasks over CPU uptime, indicating the portion of the time that the provisioned cores were utilized to run Spark tasks". It is evident that higher Efficiency values are better. We report the corresponding results when using the 1600K dataset in Fig. 7a, where the horizontal axis stands for the percentage of additional noise injected, while the vertical axis represents Efficiency Ratio. The results illustrated in these sets of experiments depict average measures of five executions.

For the PS method (dotted lines with crosses), at the beginning, Efficiency increases with noise. However, it soon starts deteriorating, indicating that cluster cores remain unused due to the global sorting featured in this method. On the other hand, PSPS (dashed line with stars) and PSPSSH (dashed-dotted line with X's) exhibit better efficiency which is almost the same, even without the injec-tion of noise. As noise is injected, efficiency increases with PSPSSH superseding PSPS.

Let is now examine what happens in terms of total CPU time, indicating the total time in seconds that the CPUs where employed, represented by the vertical axis of Fig. 7b. Again, the horizontal axis stands for the additional noise

---

[2] Available at:https://github.com/datamechanics/delight.

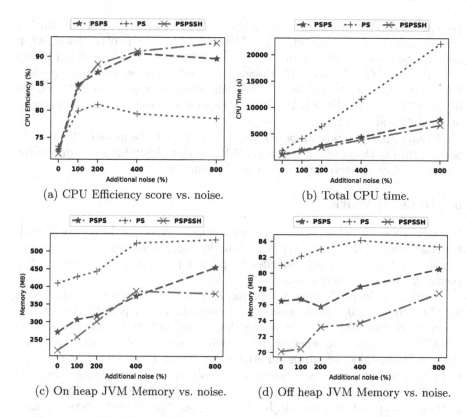

(a) CPU Efficiency score vs. noise.

(b) Total CPU time.

(c) On heap JVM Memory vs. noise.

(d) Off heap JVM Memory vs. noise.

Fig. 7. Spark engine resources utilization.

injected. We may observe that the PS measures increased time usage compared to the PSPS and PSPSSH methods, a fact which also aligns with the results of execution time we discussed earlier in this Section. In all three cases, CPU time is proportional to the additional noise injected. However, the PS method's line exhibits a steeper slope than PSPS and PSPSSH. Last but not least, we observe that PSPSSH also outperforms PSPS in terms of scalability, as it requires less overall CPU time.

Combining the observations resulting from Fig. 7a-b, we may conclude that the cluster-wide sorting employed in PS leads to a lower Efficiency Ratio and CPU time as a result of the under-utilization of CPU cores, a situation that is remedied, however, by PSPS and PSPSSH.

We will examine, now, for the same set of experiments, memory utilization. In Fig. 7c-d, we illustrate the amount of on heap and off heap JVM memory used when noise is added. We may discern that, for all approaches, increasing noise leads to increased memory consumption. On the other hand, it is easy to see that both proposed approaches, PSPS and PSPSSH, exhibit a significantly lower memory footprint compared to PS. Considering the case of no noise, for on heap JVM memory usage, PS consumes approximately 409 MB of memory on average, while PSPS manages to drop this number to 270 MB. PSPSSH further reduces memory consumption to 219 MB of RAM. On the other hand, when injecting 800% noise, PS requires at maximum 533 MB of on heap RAM, PSPS 454 MB and PSPSSH 381 MB. Moving on to off heap memory consumption, PS requires from 81 to almost 84 MB, while the consumption of PSPS ranges between 75.8 and 80 MB of RAM. PSPSSH achieves an even better performance, between 70 and 77.5 MB.

To sum up, the newly proposed methods manage to be more CPU efficient, better utilizing the cluster's resources. What is more PSPSSH also exhibits the best scalability characteristics out of all three methods.

6 Related Work

Soundex [20] is the oldest, the best known and most widely used Phonetic Encoding Algorithm [3]. More recently, MetaSoundex [18] has emerged, attempting to combine Metaphone [21] and Soundex for privacy-preserving record linkage, featuring, however, low performance.

For the problem of Privacy-Preserving Record Linkage, recent advancements may be found in [10]. Bloom filters [6,28] comprise a very popular approach in this area. Bloom filters are combined with *n-grams* and the resulting bit vectors are ANDed to determine whether they match. It has been shown that such solutions are vulnerable, requiring additional hardening measures [9]. Alternative techniques include the ones of Smith [30], who proposes encoding sensitive data into bit vectors and applying Locality Sensitive Hashing, with the drawback of increased computational cost [4]. Ranbaduge et al. [23] propose a two-step hash method where quasi-identifiers are converted into *n-grams* beforehand. However, all bit-vector based approaches cannot be indexed for fast joins, requiring blocking techniques [13] to improve efficiency.

Furthermore, in the last few years, methods based on cryptographic primitives have emerged. These methods include homomorphic encryption [7], known, however, for its high computational cost [1] and susceptibility to certain types of attacks [11], garbled circuits [2], needing to be further investigated in terms of execution time, size and reusability in this context [25] and Fuzzy Vaults [19] relying on polynomial reconstruction through interpolation.

Differential privacy has also been used in the context of privacy-preserving record linkage as a means of providing formal bounds on privacy. At the moment, solutions on differential privacy for privacy-preserving record linkage only focus on categorical and numerical attributes [24], while our work focuses on string attributes, which is the most common type of quasi-identifiers [3].

Now, when it comes to big data volumes and privacy-preserving record linkage, there are particular challenges that need to be addressed, such as improving scalability and privacy [31]. To address these challenges, the use of distributed and parallel processing engines has been extensively used in the literature. In [17], a Hadoop-based tool for defining linkage workflows including both matching and indexing steps is proposed. Karakasidis et al. [12] provide a first work utilizing Spark and Soundex. This is the work we are building upon. Karapiperis et al.

[16] use Hadoop for privacy-preserving record linkage for an LSH-based method. Franke et al. [8] use Spark and Flink for an LSH-based method. Hadoop has been outperformed by Spark, while LSH-based methods need parameter configuration. Pita et. al [22] present a first approach that exploits the Spark platform so as to create data marts for the Brazilian Public Health System using large databases from the Ministry of Health and the Ministry of Social Development and Hunger Alleviation using a Bloom filter-based method. Although providing speedup by parallelizing computation, Bloom filter problems described earlier still pertain.

7 Conclusions and Future Work

In this paper, we have presented two methods for further increasing the speedup offered by employing Spark for privacy preserving record linkage using Soundex. PSPS (Parallel Soundex, Partition-wise Shuffling) speeds up PS (Parallel Soundex) up to 3x while maintaining the same privacy characteristics. PSPSSH (Parallel Soundex, Partition-wise Shuffling, Single Hash) offers enhanced privacy characteristics and further speeds up PS, but with limitations proportional to the dataset size. Our future research directions are aimed at providing an adaptive method to trade off between PSPS and PSPSSH that will combine the advantages of both approaches.

References

1. Bonomi, L., Huang, Y., Ohno-Machado, L.: Privacy challenges and research opportunities for genomic data sharing. Nat. Genet. **52**(7), 646–654 (2020)
2. Chen, F., et al.: Perfectly secure and efficient two-party electronic-health-record linkage. IEEE Internet Comput. **22**(2), 32–41 (2018)
3. Christen, P.: Data Matching - Concepts and Techniques for Record Linkage, Entity Resolution, and Duplicate Detection. Springer, Data-Centric Systems and Applications. Springer, Heidelberg (2012). https://doi.org/10.1007/978-3-642-31164-2
4. Christen, P., Ranbaduge, T., Schnell, R.: Linking Sensitive Data - Methods and Techniques for Practical Privacy-Preserving Information Sharing. Springer, Cham (2020). https://doi.org/10.1007/978-3-030-59706-1
5. Cruz, I.F., Tamassia, R., Yao, D.: Privacy-preserving schema matching using mutual information. In: Barker, S., Ahn, G.-J. (eds.) DBSec 2007. LNCS, vol. 4602, pp. 93–94. Springer, Heidelberg (2007). https://doi.org/10.1007/978-3-540-73538-0_7
6. Durham, E., Kantarcioglu, M., Xue, Y., Toth, C., Kuzu, M., Malin, B., et al.: Composite bloom filters for secure record linkage. IEEE Trans. Knowl. Data Eng. **26**(12), 2956–2968 (2014)
7. Essex, A.: Secure approximate string matching for privacy-preserving record linkage. IEEE Trans. Inf. Forensics Secur. **14**(10), 2623–2632 (2019)
8. Franke, M., Sehili, Z., Rahm, E.: Parallel privacy-preserving record linkage using LSH-based blocking. In: 3rd International Conference on Internet of Things, Big Data and Security, pp. 195–203. SciTePress (2018)

9. Franke, M., Sehili, Z., Rohde, F., Rahm, E.: Evaluation of hardening techniques for privacy-preserving record linkage. In: 24th International Conference on Extending Database Technology, pp. 289–300. OpenProceedings.org (2021)

10. Gkoulalas-Divanis, A., Vatsalan, D., Karapiperis, D., Kantarcioglu, M.: Modern privacy-preserving record linkage techniques: An overview. IEEE Trans. Inf. Forensics Secur. **16**, 4966–4987 (2021)

11. Goodrich, M.T.: The mastermind attack on genomic data. In: 30th IEEE Symposium on Security and Privacy, pp. 204–218. IEEE Computer Society (2009)

12. Karakasidis, A., Koloniari, G.: Phonetics-based parallel privacy preserving record linkage. In: Xhafa, F., Caballé, S., Barolli, L. (eds.) 3PGCIC 2017. LNDECT, vol. 13, pp. 179–190. Springer, Cham (2018). https://doi.org/10.1007/978-3-319-69835-9_16

13. Karakasidis, A., Koloniari, G., Verykios, V.S.: Scalable blocking for privacy preserving record linkage. In: The 21st ACM SIGKDD International Conference on Knowledge Discovery and Data Mining, pp. 527–536. ACM (2015)

14. Karakasidis, A., Verykios, V.S.: Privacy preserving record linkage using phonetic codes. In: Fourth Balkan Conference in Informatics, pp. 101–106. IEEE Computer Society (2009)

15. Karakasidis, A., Verykios, V.S., Christen, P.: Fake injection strategies for private phonetic matching. In: Garcia-Alfaro, J., Navarro-Arribas, G., Cuppens-Boulahia, N., de Capitani di Vimercati, S. (eds.) DPM/SETOP -2011. LNCS, vol. 7122, pp. 9–24. Springer, Heidelberg (2012). https://doi.org/10.1007/978-3-642-28879-1_2

16. Karapiperis, D., Verykios, V.S.: A distributed near-optimal LSH-based framework for privacy-preserving record linkage. Comput. Sci. Inf. Syst. **11**(2), 745–763 (2014)

17. Kolb, L., Thor, A., Rahm, E.: Dedoop: efficient deduplication with hadoop. Proceed. VLDB Endow. **5**(12), 1878–1881 (2012)

18. Koneru, K., Varol, C.: Privacy preserving record linkage using metasoundex algorithm. In: 16th IEEE International Conference on Machine Learning and Applications, pp. 443–447. IEEE (2017)

19. Mullaymeri, X., Karakasidis, A.: Using fuzzy vaults for privacy preserving record linkage. In: The 23rd International Workshop on Design, Optimization, Languages and Analytical Processing of Big Data. CEUR Workshop Proceedings, vol. 2840, pp. 101–110. CEUR-WS.org (2021)

20. Odell, M., Russell, R.: The soundex coding system. US Patents 1261167 (1918)

21. Philips, L.: Hanging on the metaphone. Comput. Lang. **7**(12), 39–43 (1990)

22. Pita, R., Pinto, C., Melo, P., Silva, M., Barreto, M., Rasella, D.: A spark-based workflow for probabilistic record linkage of healthcare data. In: Proceedings of the Workshops of the EDBT/ICDT 2015 Joint Conference. CEUR Workshop Proceedings, vol. 1330, pp. 17–26. CEUR-WS.org (2015)

23. Ranbaduge, T., Christen, P., Schnell, R.: Secure and accurate two-step hash encoding for privacy-preserving record linkage. In: Lauw, H.W., Wong, R.C.-W., Ntoulas, A., Lim, E.-P., Ng, S.-K., Pan, S.J. (eds.) PAKDD 2020. LNCS (LNAI), vol. 12085, pp. 139–151. Springer, Cham (2020). https://doi.org/10.1007/978-3-030-47436-2_11

24. Rao, F., Cao, J., Bertino, E., Kantarcioglu, M.: Hybrid private record linkage: Separating differentially private synopses from matching records. ACM Trans. Priv. Secur. **22**(3), 1–36 (2019)

25. Saleem, A., Khan, A., Shahid, F., Alam, M., Khan, M.K.: Recent advancements in garbled computing: How far have we come towards achieving secure, efficient and reusable garbled circuits. J. Netw. Comput. Appl. **108**, 1–19 (2018)

26. Salloum, S., Dautov, R., Chen, X., Peng, P.X., Huang, J.Z.: Big data analytics on apache spark. Int. J. Data Sci. Anal. **1**(3–4), 145–164 (2016)

27. Scannapieco, M., Figotin, I., Bertino, E., Elmagarmid, A.K.: Privacy preserving schema and data matching. In: Proceedings of the ACM SIGMOD International Conference on Management of Data, pp. 653–664. ACM (2007)

28. Schnell, R., Bachteler, T., Reiher, J.: Privacy-preserving record linkage using bloom filters. BMC Med. Inform. Decis. Mak. **9**, 41 (2009)

29. Shanahan, J.G., Dai, L.: Large scale distributed data science using apache spark. In: The 21st ACM SIGKDD International Conference on Knowledge Discovery and Data Mining, pp. 2323–2324. ACM (2015)

30. Smith, D.: Secure pseudonymisation for privacy-preserving probabilistic record linkage. J. Inf. Secur. Appl. **34**, 271–279 (2017)

31. Vatsalan, D., Sehili, Z., Christen, P., Rahm, E.: Privacy-preserving record linkage for big data: current approaches and research challenges. In: Zomaya, A.Y., Sakr, S. (eds.) Handbook of Big Data Technologies, pp. 851–895. Springer, Cham (2017). https://doi.org/10.1007/978-3-319-49340-4_25

32. Vidanage, A., Ranbaduge, T., Christen, P., Schnell, R.: A taxonomy of attacks on privacy-preserving record linkage. J. Priv. Confidentiality **12**(1), jpc.764 (2022)

33. Zaharia, M., Chowdhury, M., Franklin, M.J., Shenker, S., Stoica, I.: Spark: cluster computing with working sets. In: 2nd USENIX Workshop on Hot Topics in Cloud Computing, HotCloud 2010. USENIX Association (2010)

Privacy Preserving Queries of Shortest Path Distances

Ernst Althaus[1]([✉])(iD), Stefan Funke[2], and Moritz Schrauth[1]

[1] Johannes Gutenberg-Universität Mainz, Mainz, Germany
ernst.althaus@uni-mainz.de, contact@mschrauth.de
[2] Universität Stuttgart, Stuttgart, Germany
funke@fmi.uni-stuttgart.de

Abstract. Consider a user with a very limited hardware and internet connection who wants to query a shortest path distance from a web service, but doesn't want to reveal the source and destination to the server. Using state-of-the-art methods, we show that we can privately query shortest path distances in this case, if we are allowed to use three non-cooperating servers of moderate compute and communication power. We argue that this is not possible with classical shortest path algorithms. Finally, we give some experiments showing the feasibility of the approach.

Keywords: Privacy Preserving Computation · Shortest Path · Web Service

1 Introduction

Accessing services over the world wide web endanger the privacy of the user. If a user queries a shortest path to some destination, the web service can draw the conclusion that the user plans to travel to that destination and can use this assumption e.g. to personalize advertisements. In this paper, we consider the question whether it is possible to query shortest path distances from a web service without revealing the endpoints.

Privacy preserving computations are a very active research field at the moment. For example, there is plenty of work being done trying to make machine learning methods privacy preserving (e.g. [2,3,11,14] for a few very recent papers). Most of the approaches are based either on homomorphic encryption [6] or on secret sharing approaches [7]. For both approaches there are libraries for the basic operations. Our approach is based on secret sharing.

Both methods allow at least addition and multiplication as basic operations. As all computation can be reduced to these two operations, every computable function can be evaluated privately, but a direct use of this leads to approaches that are way too slow for almost all interesting functions. Hence, there is a lot of work to find approaches for more advanced basic functions that can be used in different applications.

The methods get very inefficient if we want to keep private which variables are involved in the computation, e.g. a variable that is stored in an array and

L. Foschini and S. Kontogiannis (Eds.): ALGOCLOUD 2022, LNCS 13799, pp. 94–101, 2023.
https://doi.org/10.1007/978-3-031-33437-5_6

indirectly accessed by a private index. Accessing the value of such a variable requires a private information retrieval (explained below). As such an operation is very frequent in Dijkstra's algorithm, we will argue that it can not be made privacy preserving while remaining efficient. Hence, in order to make shortest path queries privacy preserving, we need other, more suitable algorithms to compute the shortest path. Most efficient methods to compute shortest path in road networks are hub-label approaches [1], contraction hierarchies [9] or combinations of both [5]. As hub-label approaches have the smallest query time, we use these in the paper.

In the following, we will assume that the graph in which the shortest path queries take place is publicly known, but the user has very little memory and compute power and hence can not store the graph and/or compute shortest path in the graph. Furthermore, we assume that the connection to the web service is slow. To achieve acceptable query times, we will make use of three servers in the so called honest-but-curious setting, i.e. the servers stick to the protocol and do not cooperate to harm the privacy of the user. Still, they use all information they get through the protocol to learn the query of the user and hence, we have to ensure that the endpoints of the query are not revealed.

In our setting, two servers will store the graph and both compute hub-labels for it (explained in more detail later). These servers are called the main servers. A third server is used to lower the amount of traffic between the user and the main servers and is called the helper server.

The rest of the paper is organized as follows. In Sect. 2, we give some background on secret sharing and hub-label approaches. Our approach is presented in detail in Sect. 3. Finally, we give some experimental results in Sect. 4 and conclude the paper.

2 Background and Related Work

2.1 Secret Sharing

In secret sharing approaches, the input data and the intermediate results for the computations are not stored explicitly at some servers, but for each number, the servers get some shares that together can be used to reconstruct the number, but look as random numbers individually. The most simple approach is the additive secret sharing in $\mathbb{Z}_p$ for a prime number p with exactly three servers s_1, s_2 and s_3. To share a number x, each server gets a share $x_1, \ldots, x_3$ such that $x_1 + x_2 + x_3 \equiv x \mod p$. To add two numbers x and y, the servers can simply add their shares. Notice that no communication is necessary for an addition. This is different for the multiplication, which can be done as follows. Server s_1 sends its shares to s_2, server s_2 to s_3 and server s_3 to s_1 so that each server has now two of the three shares. Server s_1 computes $z_1 := x_1 y_1 + x_2 y_1 + x_1 y_2$ while s_2 and s_3 perform symmetric computations. Notice that $xy = z_1 + z_2 + z_3 \mod p$. After a multiplication, a so-call *resharing* is done, e.g. by creating random shares for zero (which we do not explain here) and adding them, so that the shares of the result are distributed uniformly.

A private information retrieval (PIR) protocol enables a user to request the u-th entry of a public database $D[1..n]$ without revealing u. There are no privacy concerns for the database. PIR is very well studied (see e.g. [8]) and it is known that in the two server setting, a traffic of $\Theta(\sqrt{n})$ is sufficient and necessary. This is done by partitioning the database in $\sqrt{n}$ blocks and querying a block with the following approach to access an element with linear traffic. To access $D[u]$ out of an array $D[0, \ldots, n]$, the user generates an n-bit vector h_1 and sends h_1 to server s_1 and $h_2 := h_1 \oplus e_u$ to server s_2, where e_u is the u-th unit vector. Server s_i computes $d_i := \oplus_{w | e_w \oplus h_i \neq 0} D[w]$ and sends d_i to the user. The user computes $D[u]$ as $d := d_1 \oplus d_2$. Notice that h_1 and h_2 are bit-vectors which were chosen uniformly at random and hence no server learns anything on which entry is accessed. Furthermore, d equals $D[u]$ as $D[u]$ appears in d exactly once whereas all other $D[v]$ appear exactly twice or not at all.

In our setting, we directly query an entry without building blocks, as each data point is quite large and the amount of traffic for the user is minimized without building blocks, as explained in Sect. 3.

2.2   Infeasibility of Dijktra's Algorithm

If we do not preprocess the graph, Dijkstra's algorithm to compute shortest path distances is the most commonly used method if there are no privacy concerns. In this section, we argue that this algorithm can not made privacy preserving with current hardware even for relatively small graphs. As an example, we will consider a graph with 1 million vertices.

Dijkstra's algorithm iterates over all vertices in increasing distance to the source of the query. For each vertex, its adjacency list is scanned and distances are updated. As we want to preserve the privacy of the source, the servers are not allowed to get any information on the order in which the vertices are handled. Hence, in order to iterate over an adjacency list, one has to do a PIR over the graph. We ignore all communication that is needed to update distances and to query the vertex with smallest distance. Nevertheless, this iteration has to be done for all vertices (even if the target is found early, we can not stop the iteration as otherwise the servers could exclude some source-destination pairs), and therefore we have 1 million PIR-rounds. Even for a network with infinite bandwidth and a latency of 1ms, a single query would take more than 15min.

Notice that the Bellman-Ford-algorithm can be made privacy preserving very easily as the order in which the edges are traversed can be made public, but this algorithm is too slow to compute shortest path distances even in the non-private setting and the number of rounds would be at least the number of vertices of the graph, too.

2.3   Hub-Label Approaches

In this section, we very briefly restate the hub-label approach to compute shortest path distances (see e.g. [1] for details).

Consider a directed graph $G = (V := \{0, \ldots, n-1\}, E)$. For a vertex $u \in V$, a forward label $D^+[u]$ for u is a list of pairs (v, d) where $v \in V$ and d is the length of the shortest path from u to v. A backward label $D^-[u]$ for u is a list of pairs (v, d) such that d is the distance from v to u. A set $(D^+[u], D^-[u])_{u \in V}$ is a hub-labeling for G, if for all pairs of vertices u and v, there is a vertex $w \in D^+[u] \cap D^-[v]$ such that the distance from u to v is $d(u, w) + d(w, v)$.

Given a hub-labeling, shortest path distances can be computed almost trivially. Given a pair of vertices u, v, we compute the minimum value of $d(u, w) + d(w, v)$ for all $w \in D^+[u] \cap D^-[v]$. Storing the hub-labels in increasing index, this can be done in time linear in the size of the larger hub-label.

Interestingly, there are methods to compute hub-labelings of real world graphs in reasonable time such that all hub-labels remain reasonably small (see e.g. [1]).

2.4 Existing Approaches for Privacy-Preserving Computation of Shortest Path

There are several previous approaches to compute shortest paths under different privacy constraints. However, all we are aware of consider only significantly smaller graphs (i.e. at most a few thousand of vertices and not several million).

We assume that the graph is public, while most existing approaches assume that either the complete graph or at least the weights of the edges are private [4,13]. To hide the length of the edges in our approach, the computation of the minimum of $d(u, w) + d(w, v)$ for all $w \in D^+[u] \cap D^-[v]$ would have to be computed privately, for which many methods are known (see e.g. [10])

Many approaches are based on a computation of all-pairs shortest paths [12,16] and hence can not scale to graphs with several million vertices. The setting in [16] is similar to ours, i.e. a user who is concerned with their privacy and several honest-but-curious servers computing the shortest path, but they do not report experimental results.

Anagreth et al. [4] proposed a method that is based on a parallelization of the Bellman-Ford algorithm. Their approach is based on secure multiparty computation and experimental results are reported for graphs with up to 10.000 vertices and 1.5 million edges, using several days of parallel computation. For the serial version, a running time of about a day is reported for a graph with 900 vertices and 20.000 edges.

Wu et al. [15] guarantee the privacy of user and the weights of edges held by the server. They report on experimental results of city maps of big US cities with up to 7000 vertices. The running time for a distance query takes between four and five seconds in this graph, giving also the predecessor vertex. As the maximal number of edges of a shortest path in this graph is 165, we can repeat the approach with the predecessors 165 times (the user is not allowed to stop early as this would reveal the number of edges on the shortest path of the user query) to get the path itself. The total time was reported to be 784 seconds. In this paper, we only compute the length of the shortest path, but clearly, we could use the same approach to obtain the path itself. However, the maximal number of edges on a shortest path is even larger in the graphs we are considering.

3   Privately Querying Shortest Path Distances Using Hub-Labels

We assume that the two main servers store the graph $G = (\{0, \ldots, n-1\}, E)$ and possible hub-labels $D^+[0, \ldots, n-1]$ and $D^-[0, \ldots, n-1]$. The number n of vertices of the graph and the bit length m of the longest hub-label is assumed to be known by all servers and the user.

We assume that the user knows u and v. If he only has a geographic location or an address, getting u and v requires a further PIR operation for each endpoint.

From the discussion above, to compute the shortest path distance between u and v, the user has to do a PIR for $D^+[u]$ and $D^-[v]$ and a trivial computation with $D^+[u]$ and $D^-[v]$. Directly using the PIR protocol as explained above would require the user to send two bit-vectors of n bits. However, this can be reduced in the following way. Let h be the helper server and s_1 and s_2 be the two main servers.

The main idea is to cyclically shift the indices of the vertices by a random number r. The helper computes the vectors h_1 and h_2 for the shifted index (without getting r) and the main servers get the shifting r and either h_1 or h_2 for the query with shifted index.

Consider the source u of the query. Instead of computing and sending h_1 and h_2, the user generates a random number $r \in \mathbb{Z}_n$ and sends $r + u \mod n$ to h and r to servers s_1 and s_2. Here we slightly abuse notation and interpret $x \mod n$ as the integer number between 0 and $n-1$. The helper h generates a random n-bit vector h_1, computes $h_2 := h_1 \oplus e_{r+u \mod n}$ and sends h_i to s_i. The servers compute $d_i := \oplus_{w|e_{w+r \mod n} \oplus h_i \neq 0} D^+[w]$ and send d_i to the user. The user computes the hub-label $D^+[u]$ as $d_1 \oplus d_2$.

For the destination v, we generate a new random number and replace u by v and D^+ by D^- in the computation. As the helper only gets the randomly shifted index of the query, it does not learn the query itself. The main servers get the random shift, but h_1 or h_2 do not give any additional information and hence, they can not infer any information on the query. The correctness directly follows from the correctness of the PIR protocol.

Notice that the user sends two $\log n$-bit numbers to each of the servers and gets two hub-labels in two shares each, hence only $4m$ bits have to be transferred. It only has to compute two xor's of the shares and scan the hub-labels. This is a feasible communication and computation even for very restricted users.

The helper server gets two $\log n$-bit numbers and sends four n-bit vectors it generates randomly. Even for large graphs, this is feasible with a reasonable internet connection of the helper.

The main servers get two n-bit vectors and send two shares of hub-labels, which is feasible with a reasonable internet connection. The main bottleneck is the computation of the shares d_i for the source and the target of the query. For that, roughly half of the hub-labels have to be xor'ed. In the next section, we report on the time required.

Table 1. We give the time in seconds, the size and the bit-length of the longest hub-label for different graphs. These numbers were known from previous papers on the hub-label approach. In the last column, we give the average time with standard deviation of a shortest path query for our approach.

Instance	Graph		Preprocessing			Query
	$|V|$	$|E|$	Time (in hh:mm:ss)	Size	m	Time ± sd (in seconds)
Germany	25,115,477	91,898,003	55:44	38,168MB	15,488	3.963 ± 0.0549
Great-Britain	23,464,670	82,354,087	26:02	37,104MB	16,128	3.833 ± 0.0376
Switzerland	4,548,106	16,513,098	06:12	3,736MB	8,768	0.942 ± 0.0459
South-America	62,562,908	252,966,975	01:03:49	75,224MB	20,288	9.275 ± 0.0577

4   Experiments

We report the running times of preprocessing the graph and handling queries for different graphs of road networks. To measure the query time, we repeatedly selected two random vertices for 100 times. We believe that this number of repetitions is sufficient, as the query time does not depend on the source and target vertex at all. We implemented the approach in the Rust programming language (www.rust-lang.org) and let all parties run on different docker (https://www.docker.com/) on the same computer, containing an AMD Ryzen 5 5600x CPU (6 × 3.7 GHz) with 128GB of RAM. As there is only very little communication, we ignored the fact that our network is much faster than one may expect from a web service. Running the servers on different machines would require to either run the preprocessing on two machines or copy the hub-labels from one machine to an other. The query times should be roughly halved in this case. We encode each integer number by 32bit, i.e. we waste some bits for smaller graphs.

Table 1 shows the results of our experiments in terms of preprocessing time, size of the hub-labels and query time. The most computation time was spent on the xor over half of the hub-labels of the two main servers. Nevertheless, the approach is feasible for all graphs where the hub-labels fit into the main memory. The main bottleneck is the memory requirement of the hub-label approach.

5   Conclusion

We showed that using state-of-the-art methods for computing shortest path allows to privately query shortest path distances even in relatively large graphs using known methods to privately query databases.

In future work, we plan to extend the method to enable the user to compute the path itself and not only its distance. Furthermore, we want to investigate, whether approaches for the shortest path problem that need less memory can be made privacy preserving while remaining efficient.

References

1. Abraham, I., Delling, D., Goldberg, A.V., Werneck, R.F.: Hierarchical hub labelings for shortest paths. In: Epstein, L., Ferragina, P. (eds.) ESA 2012. LNCS, vol. 7501, pp. 24–35. Springer, Heidelberg (2012). https://doi.org/10.1007/978-3-642-33090-2_4
2. Adams, S., et al.: Privacy-preserving training of tree ensembles over continuous data. Proc. Priv. Enhancing Technol. **2022**(2), 205–226 (2022). https://doi.org/10.2478/popets-2022-0042
3. Akavia, A., Leibovich, M., Resheff, Y.S., Ron, R., Shahar, M., Vald, M.: Privacy-preserving decision trees training and prediction. IACR Cryptol. ePrint Arch. 768 (2021). https://eprint.iacr.org/2021/768
4. Anagreh, M., Laud, P., Vainikko, E.: Privacy-preserving parallel computation of shortest path algorithms with low round complexity. In: Mori, P., Lenzini, G., Furnell, S. (eds.) Proceedings of the 8th International Conference on Information Systems Security and Privacy, ICISSP 2022, Online Streaming, February 9–11, 2022, pp. 37–47. SCITEPRESS (2022). https://doi.org/10.5220/0010775700003120
5. Bahrdt, D., Funke, S., Makolli, S., Proissl, C.: Distance closures: unifying search- and lookup-based shortest path speedup techniques. In: Phillips, C.A., Speckmann, B. (eds.) Proceedings of the Symposium on Algorithm Engineering and Experiments, ALENEX 2022, Alexandria, VA, USA, 9–10 January 2022, pp. 1–12. SIAM (2022). https://doi.org/10.1137/1.9781611977042.1
6. Chatterjee, A., Aung, K.M.M.: Fully homomorphic encryption in real world applications. Computer Architecture and Design Methodologies, vol. 295. Springer, Cham (2021). https://doi.org/10.1007/978-981-13-6393-1
7. Cramer, R., Damgård, I., Nielsen, J.B.: Secure Multiparty Computation and Secret Sharing. Cambridge University Press (2015), http://www.cambridge.org/de/academic/subjects/computer-science/cryptography-cryptology-and-coding/secure-multiparty-computation-and-secret-sharing?format=HB&isbn=9781107043053
8. Demmler, D., Herzberg, A., Schneider, T.: RAID-PIR: practical multi-server PIR. In: Ahn, G., Oprea, A., Safavi-Naini, R. (eds.) Proceedings of the 6th edition of the ACM Workshop on Cloud Computing Security, CCSW 2014, Scottsdale, Arizona, USA, November 7, 2014, pp. 45–56. ACM (2014). https://doi.org/10.1145/2664168.2664181
9. Geisberger, R., Sanders, P., Schultes, D., Vetter, C.: Exact routing in large road networks using contraction hierarchies. Transp. Sci. **46**(3), 388–404 (2012). https://doi.org/10.1287/trsc.1110.0401
10. Goss, K., Jiang, W.: Efficient and constant-rounds secure comparison through dynamic groups and asymmetric computations. IACR Cryptol. ePrint Arch. p. 179 (2018). http://eprint.iacr.org/2018/179
11. Lee, J., et al.: Privacy-preserving machine learning with fully homomorphic encryption for deep neural network. IEEE Access **10**, 30039–30054 (2022). https://doi.org/10.1109/ACCESS.2022.3159694
12. Ramezanian, S., Meskanen, T., Niemi, V.: Privacy-protecting algorithms for digraph shortest path queries. Int. J. Embed. Real Time Commun. Syst. **10**(3), 86–100 (2019). https://doi.org/10.4018/IJERTCS.2019070106
13. Sealfon, A.: Shortest paths and distances with differential privacy. In: Milo, T., Tan, W. (eds.) Proceedings of the 35th ACM SIGMOD-SIGACT-SIGAI Symposium on Principles of Database Systems, PODS 2016, San Francisco, CA, USA, June 26 - July 01, 2016, pp. 29–41. ACM (2016). https://doi.org/10.1145/2902251.2902291

14. Tan, S., Knott, B., Tian, Y., Wu, D.J.: Cryptgpu: Fast privacy-preserving machine learning on the GPU. In: 42nd IEEE Symposium on Security and Privacy, SP 2021, San Francisco, CA, USA, 24–27 May 2021. pp. 1021–1038. IEEE (2021). https://doi.org/10.1109/SP40001.2021.00098

15. Wu, D.J., Zimmerman, J., Planul, J., Mitchell, J.C.: Privacy-preserving shortest path computation. In: 23rd Annual Network and Distributed System Security Symposium, NDSS 2016, San Diego, California, USA, February 21–24, 2016. The Internet Society (2016). http://wp.internetsociety.org/ndss/wp-content/uploads/sites/25/2017/09/privacy-preserving-shortest-path-computation.pdf

16. Xi, Y., Schwiebert, L., Shi, W.: Privacy preserving shortest path routing with an application to navigation. Pervasive Mob. Comput. **13**, 142–149 (2014). https://doi.org/10.1016/j.pmcj.2013.06.002

Author Index

L. Foschini and S. Kontogiannis (Eds.): ALGOCLOUD 2022, LNCS 13799, p. 103, 2023.
https://doi.org/10.1007/978-3-031-33437-5

Printed in the United States
by Baker & Taylor Publisher Services